About Island Press

Since 1984, the nonprofit organization Island Press has been stimulating, shaping, and communicating ideas that are essential for solving environmental problems worldwide. With more than 1,000 titles in print and some 30 new releases each year, we are the nation's leading publisher on environmental issues. We identify innovative thinkers and emerging trends in the environmental field. We work with world-renowned experts and authors to develop cross-disciplinary solutions to environmental challenges.

Island Press designs and executes educational campaigns, in conjunction with our authors, to communicate their critical messages in print, in person, and online using the latest technologies, innovative programs, and the media. Our goal is to reach targeted audiences—scientists, policy makers, environmental advocates, urban planners, the media, and concerned citizens—with information that can be used to create the framework for long-term ecological health and human well-being.

Island Press gratefully acknowledges major support from The Bobolink Foundation, Caldera Foundation, The Curtis and Edith Munson Foundation, The Forrest C. and Frances H. Lattner Foundation, The JPB Foundation, The Kresge Foundation, The Summit Charitable Foundation, Inc., and many other generous organizations and individuals.

The opinions expressed in this book are those of the author(s) and do not necessarily reflect the views of our supporters.

Recast Your City

Artisan Businesses Bring a Neighborhood to Life

Recast Your City

How to Save Your Downtown
with Small-Scale Manufacturing

ILANA PREUSS

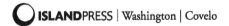

ISLANDPRESS | Washington | Covelo

Library of Congress Control Number: 2020946283

All Island Press books are printed on environmentally responsible materials.

Manufactured in the United States of America

10 9 8 7 6 5 4 3

All chapter illustrations were created by Mary Koger at Crow Insight, LLC.

Keywords: artisanal business, downtown redevelopment, economic resilience, inclusive economic prosperity, locally owned business, Main Street, makerspace, microenterprise, micromanufacturing, neighborhood center, Opportunity Zone, public participation, real estate development, shared kitchen, shared textile space, shared woodshop, small-scale manufacturing, wealth gap

To my parents, Ruth and Peter, for teaching everyone in your lives to believe in themselves and in the worth of other people, for teaching me to use a drill and fix things, and for teaching me that we each have a responsibility to do good in the world. Thank you.

Contents

Small-Scale Manufacturing: The Secret Sauce

CHAPTER 1

What It Means
to Recast Your City

In 2019, I WAS IN A VAN FULL OF RESIDENTS and visitors being driven down the old neighborhood main street of McComb-Veazey, a historically Black and Creole neighborhood in Lafayette, Louisiana. At one intersection, Tina Bingham, the driver, pointed in different directions and explained, "That used to be our grocery store, but it closed ten years ago and is a hair supply store now. Over there, we used to have an old bank building, but the property owner let it sit empty for so long it became a safety hazard and was bulldozed last year. And this old car dealership building with the glass front right along the street edge just sits empty and is used for storage." In every direction we looked, we saw vacant lots or buildings that had seen better days.

This neighborhood had once been home to zydeco music legends, markets, and churches and had been a cultural center for Creole foods. It was clear from Bingham's description of the old main street that it had been the heart of the neighborhood, a place where people came together. Over time, this area had been cut off from downtown and the neighboring areas by new railroad tracks, then by the state highway, and now by the threat of a new elevated highway. There had been little investment coming to the area for a long time.

Now, though, neighborhood leaders are working hard to change things for the better. Bingham, who leads the McComb-Veazey neighborhood association and serves as the community development director for the local chapter of Habitat for Humanity, has brought those two organizations together to redevelop delinquent properties and create new homes and community spaces in the neighborhood. This old main street was next on her list—the residents didn't own any of that property and had lost control over that space a long time ago.

I was there to find ways to get locally owned small-scale manufacturers into these spaces to bring this main street back—for the neighborhood and by the neighborhood. On our tour, we met neighborhood business owners offering amazing Creole food such as boudin and pickled okra but who had no place to grow, and no place to get business development support. Bingham believed in the value of the skills of her neighbors and the history of the place, and she knew that this street could be so much more. She recognized that small-scale manufacturing businesses—business that make products—could help bring the neighborhood back to life.

The Secret Sauce: Small-Scale Manufacturing

Small-scale manufacturing businesses create a tangible product—in any material—that can be replicated or packaged; my catch-all is "hot sauce, handbags, and hardware." The business can be all about technology (for example, a supply chain business that uses 3D printers to supply parts for the Department of Defense) or can be artisan (for example, a consumer-facing business that handcrafts leather handbags). It can be food-based (beer or chocolate anyone?), or it can be food material–based (all-natural lotions). It can sell direct to consumers, sell wholesale to retailers, or sell into business-to-business supply chains.

Such businesses are considered small scale because of their number of employees and the amount of space they need. Small-scale manufacturing businesses have fewer than fifty employees; most of the time, they have fewer than twenty. Their space needs are smaller, too; they generally need less than 5,000 square feet of space, and most need less than 1,000 to 2,000 square feet. They can operate in storefronts and smaller spaces that are not considered "manufacturing" and in general, large, distant industrial spaces don't serve their needs because of their small space requirements. In addition, these businesses are modern manufacturing and are most often quiet, clean, and great neighbors.

Small-scale manufacturing businesses help us create thriving places, with business ownership opportunities and good-paying jobs that other business types cannot fulfill. They are the hidden gems in the economic development strategy and downtown reinvestment efforts of every place (yes, I really mean *every* place).

You already have some type of small-scale manufacturing business in your community, and as you learn more about these businesses in this book, you may start to notice them. One example is Katie Stack's shop, Stitch & Rivet in Northeast Washington, DC. There, you can walk in and see three employees busy at their sewing machines. Little pieces of leather are neatly piled on the table corners, and the sound of the machines makes the air hum with activity. The front of the small shop is filled with Stack's leather and waxed canvas bags alongside items from complementary producers—some jewelry, funny gift cards, and other small items that round out the shop. It is easy to see all the activity because this business is in an 800-square-foot microstorefront alongside other small producers in a real estate development project called the Art Walk at Monroe Street Market, NE.

Stitch & Rivet is one of a few dozen shops along this walkway. These businesses are an essential part of what makes this project work: they fill a pedestrian walkway with active storefronts that you can't find anywhere else in the city.

These kinds of product businesses—called small-scale manufacturing—are a critical part of what makes local real estate and economic development work. I often call them hidden gems because they are in every community. The owners are working hard, with their heads down, and are rarely brought into discussions about downtown and business development opportunities, yet they are essential engines to local economies.

Tell Me More!

These businesses are all over the United States. I mean it. They are everywhere—in homes, storefronts, corners of warehouse space, coworking offices, and garages. In some cases, they are a second or third source of income for a household; in others, they are scaling businesses expanding throughout national and international markets.

These businesses are growing in new ways because of e-commerce. Many are native to the internet; others are legacy businesses making the transition.

Throughout this book, I use the terms *downtown* and *main street* to refer to any specific place you want to make great. To become a thriving place, however, each place needs to be valued and supported, and small-scale manufacturing businesses are essential to creating a thriving place with businesses that benefit the community. These businesses help diversify the tenant base in our downtown or neighborhood main street, and they also make our local economies and markets more inclusive and resilient. They help a place feel valued and allow more people to contribute to the success of main street and the local business community.

These businesses offer an opportunity to build stronger connections between people, increase the economic resiliency of the neighborhood, and create more wealth building opportunity for more people in the community. Here's why those pieces are important.

Connection

People crave connections to one another. Even in the age of COVID-19, we try to find ways to safely connect, celebrate, and build community both online and in person. Small-scale manufacturing businesses give us a reason to come together.

They are the vendors at our festivals and farmers' markets showcasing their products and making people proud of what is made in their community. They are also the "cool factor"—you can see something made in person and you won't find that business anywhere else. These business owners welcome the opportunity to come together, procure materials from one another, and attract other producers to the area.

Small-scale manufacturing businesses on main street and at festivals make people proud because they see their neighbors showcasing their skills. These businesses can fill storefronts on an empty main street and attract foot traffic (people love seeing stuff made), even while earning most of their revenue from online sales. Successful small-scale manufacturing businesses attract more business owners because entrepreneurs want to be around other entrepreneurs.

Resiliency

Economies are stronger when they are diverse. This diversity means that the community is not completely dependent on one sector (like tourism) to bring in all the local revenue, but can be supported by other parts of the economy as well. Cities with a diverse set of businesses can weather market changes more successfully and are less likely to lose their growing businesses to other cities or countries.

Even during the COVID-19 shutdowns and pauses, having a diversity of businesses allowed some places to continue to build revenue while others were closed. The Baltimore makerspace Opens Works closed at the start of COVID-19, but quickly reopened to become an essential producer of personal protection equipment that local hospitals desperately needed. Small-scale manufacturing businesses add a sector to the local economic development strategy that helps expand that diversity. They are there in the community and might be able to grow or hire more local employees with the right business development programs.

Community Wealth Building

Today, the power and energy behind local small businesses are more important than ever. Local efforts to buy from small businesses exploded during the COVID-19 shutdowns, bringing more and more people to focus on the importance of these businesses as the backbone of our local economies. Small-scale manufacturing businesses expand this opportunity.

Residents are proud to see these businesses create and sell products. The product businesses can access a strong local market alongside a global market through the internet. As more people gravitate toward unique and custom products online, artisan businesses grow in power, and dollars spent on them are increasing.[1] The power to build community wealth pairs with the national interest in unique products, allowing these business owners to bring revenue into the community from far away. Local residents can use their skills, be business owners, build community wealth, and retain what is special about the neighborhood's culture with these businesses.

More Economic Opportunity

Small-scale manufacturing businesses can make a major difference to help more people create economic opportunities, regardless of education or background. This business sector often includes many people who have been excluded from opportunities in the past. Someone who has an entrepreneurial spirit and the ability to make something can become a business owner; they just need the right support and the right space in town to become a thriving addition to the business community. Small-scale manufacturing businesses are found in every part of our communities and include people across racial, ethnic, immigrant, and income types. This kind of entrepreneurship can help families create economic opportunity for themselves and the people around them. Small-scale manufacturing businesses often hire from within the community and on average pay 50 to 100 percent more than retail or service jobs.[2]

Who They Are and Where They Go

What are these businesses, and what kind of space do they use? Here are a few examples to illustrate some of the variety and the terms used to define the different kinds of businesses, starting with the smallest and scaling up.

Artisan Businesses and Microenterprises

Artisan businesses are stand-alone businesses that produce goods, often by hand or with a small set of tools. They have a few defining characteristics: they are full-time producers, they are generally a sole proprietor business or have one to five employees, and they sell their goods online or at local markets.

These businesses may be technology and hardware based, such as Small Batch Assembly in Reston, Virginia, which creates custom electronic components. Or they may make and sell artisan consumer products, such as Stitch & Rivet in Washington, DC, the business that produces leather bags mentioned earlier. Or they could be a family food business, such as a boudin wholesale and retail company in Lafayette, Louisiana.

You have probably seen these businesses in your community. Think of the holiday markets that popped up in your community (before COVID-19). Many of those vendors are from your community. They might be part-time producers working nights and weekends to create that product, or they might be full-time businesses growing out of their home. These vendor businesses often make jewelry, bags, candles, or other consumer products.

Based on interviews conducted by Recast City (my firm; more below), we also know that many of these business owners would love to scale up but do not have access to business training courses or mentors in product businesses or have affordable space to help them succeed and grow. The businesses that are starting to scale up often lease 400 to 800 square feet of space. They may prefer interior spaces for production-only use, or they may be great microretail street-front tenants and produce in the back half of their open retail space. They also may choose to do all their production at home, even as a full-time business. Space is expensive, and profit comes first. When they have the right support, however, these businesses can be the pipeline of small-business growth, job creation, and wealth building within your community.

Artisan businesses can bring a street front to life as a group of micro-retailers or as temporary vendors for festival and holiday markets. They can also share existing larger spaces, either as part of larger food hall projects or within urban industrial properties. That is where they start.

Scaling Micromanufacturing

Scaling micromanufacturing businesses are those starting to grow. They have dedicated production space and more tools of their own. They generally have five to twenty employees and often sell through wholesale outlets, as well as online or at local markets.

These producers generally need 1,000 to 5,000 square feet of space. Their businesses may be producing custom-designed screen-printed shirts, such as Gorilla Joe Printing Co. in Youngstown, Ohio, or focus on custom consumer products, such as Harper's Naturals in Knoxville, Tennessee. The small-manufacturing businesses may be in textiles with their own cut-and-sew team for contract production, such as Sew Love in South Bend, Indiana, or create and package new dessert food products, such as Whisked in Capital Heights, Maryland, just outside Washington, DC.

The businesses that get to this stage jumped major hurdles to get there. Not only did they create a successful business with a strong revenue model, but they also they saved up or qualified for access to capital to build out a space with production equipment. This step is much more difficult than just adding more people with computers to a tech company. Micromanufacturing growth means thousands of dollars of equipment to help the business increase efficiency and output. And like artisan businesses, these businesses are often going it alone, with little or no mentorship or support from the local business community.

Some of these businesses will not want retail frontage and will select existing industrial districts or back-of-the-building options for space. Others might be wonderful storefront users, such as Zeke's Coffee in Baltimore, Maryland, and Washington, DC, which has a coffee shop at the street front and production in the rear, with wholesale distribution to the region out the back door.

Production at Scale

Small-scale manufacturing includes those businesses producing at scale for broad distribution. In this classification, the producers top out at about fifty employees, but some of these businesses continue to expand in the same space. These businesses generally use 5,000 to 30,000 square feet of space. The maximum size of the business will be most dependent on the size of spaces in the community.

These businesses include coffee roasters, such as Pan American Coffee Company in Hoboken, New Jersey, and distilleries or breweries, such as Rhinegeist in Cincinnati, Ohio. The range of businesses also includes full-scale design production, such as the custom wallpaper and art from Studio Printworks in Hoboken, New Jersey, with employees who hand silkscreen one-of-a-kind wallpaper for the New York City market.

One example shows what these businesses can mean to a neighborhood. The business owners of Rhinegeist Brewery purchased their building after their first few very successful years. They bought an old brewery in the Cincinnati Brewery District and filled the 120,000-square-foot building with a mix of brewing capacity, taproom, and community space. They knew that people craved a place to come together, and they wanted to be that place. (The day I visited, the community space was set up for indoor whiffle ball!) The essential part of this type of business is that it can still fit into the fabric of the neighborhood and into existing buildings to help reenergize the local economy and the people who live there.

Many of the production-at-scale businesses work with major brands or distributors and only operate in wholesale. They will not need the million square feet of space at the edge of town, and they will want to be a part of a community of producers. Others, such as Rhinegeist Brewery, purposefully become community gathering places or attractions for other product businesses to locate nearby. Breweries are now anchors for main streets and neighborhood centers, such as Burlington Beer Works in Burlington, North Carolina, a cooperative brewery on the town's main street launched by two thousand local residents.

In all these cases, the production stays in the city, employs people from the community, and attracts other business creators to the place.

Shared Kitchen, Shared Woodshop, and Shared Textile Space

Shared commercial kitchen, woodshop, textile, or production spaces provide access to space and tools to local small producers for a fee or with a sublease. These shops are often focused on tools within one industry, such as a health-inspected, commercial kitchen for food production that a small business can rent by the hour or a well-outfitted woodshop accessed by a set of subtenants who share the tools. These spaces generally range from 2,000 to 15,000 square feet or larger.

These shared spaces are not generally open to the public. Startups and existing small producers may apply or lease from the primary tenant. Spaces like CommonWealth Kitchen in Dorchester, Massachusetts, a mission-driven nonprofit commercial shared kitchen, focuses on startup and growth support for Latina and Black women and other entrepreneurs who are underrepresented in the regional business community. The space provides training, kitchen space, and connections to the food-product market in the Boston area to help more people launch and grow resilient small businesses.

Some places, such as the Osborn Design & Craft space in Indianapolis, Indiana, have shared woodshops. Osborn Design & Craft is a space leased by one business but shared with a number of subtenants who pay to share the space and access the woodshop tools. This setup reduces the cost of the space for the primary tenant and gives the subtenants access to better tools than they could afford individually.

Models like The Garden in Alexandria, Virginia, offer small-business owners access to many big tools, such as CNCs (computer-controlled cutting machines), laser cutters (for even thicker materials), 3D printing (also known as additive manufacturing), and welding. In many ways, the space is set up similar to a makerspace, but in this case, it is only available to small businesses that join as members as opposed to being open to the public.

These businesses and spaces help smaller businesses launch faster and grow more efficiently because they do not have to invest in these tools on their own. Growth in commercial shared kitchens is the easiest one to notice, but each of these kinds of spaces is the launch pad for many other small businesses and operate as key parts of a growing product business ecosystem.

Makerspace

Makerspaces are community centers with access to shared tools. These spaces generally range in size from 3,000 to 35,000 square feet. They provide public access to a combination of production equipment and offer classes that teach people how to design, prototype, and create tangible items that you may not usually make at home. These spaces are open to hobbyists, people who want to learn how to use a tool for fun, and anyone else from the community. The space may provide workforce development programming or startup classes, but that is location dependent. Many makerspaces are not necessarily business focused since they are open to the public. They often focus on access to maker education versus business development.

In a makerspace, people access the space by paying a monthly membership fee (like a gym) or paying for a specific class. These spaces often offer sets of tools in textiles, wood, metal, 3D printing, and CNC routers. In many cases, these spaces may overlap in the types of tools provided in a shared business space, but the makerspace is open to everyone. It may be located in a library as part of the city's services (check out Cincinnati's makerspace in its central library), or it may be a stand-alone nonprofit organization that is mission driven to increase access to maker education in a community. The spaces that operate as nonprofits, such as Artisan's Asylum in Somerville, Massachusetts, and Open Works in Baltimore, Maryland, become centers of the product community.

Open Works, with 34,000 square feet and tools running from sewing machines to welding, industrial 3D printers, and everything in the middle, is one of the largest makerspaces in the United States. The space runs product business startup classes, works with the surrounding neighborhood to bring youth into the space to learn about making and teach entrepreneurship to teens, and offers up a coworking space with dedicated desks for people who want to have a permanent space to work on their project. The space is used by small-product business owners, artists, robotics clubs, and hobbyists from throughout the Baltimore region. When COVID-19 hit, Open Works immediately turned into a personal protective equipment production space, working with partners throughout the region to churn out thousands of face shields for the surrounding health community.

Some communities invest in makerspaces as part of a school district, as in Albemarle County, Virginia, or a community college, as in Columbia, Missouri. In Albemarle County, all the high schools have makerspaces with advanced manufacturing capabilities, both to allow the students to create projects of their own and to provide training for manufacturing jobs in the region. The Moberly Area Community College in Columbia has a successful advanced manufacturing and technician certification program and has partnered with the local improvement district (The Loop) to create a makerspace that will be open to the public and its students.

Makerspaces are great assets to a neighborhood and can be an amenity to real estate projects and economic development strategies. These spaces often operate with a focus on community and youth education, workforce development, or small-business growth. To serve the needs of its community, each space has a different focus.

I'm guessing that you are starting to see the benefit of small-scale manufacturing businesses to your downtown and local economic development, but let's be clear about why all this is important.

Small-scale manufacturing businesses help people feel valued and help us see the value in the places in our community. They help us create more opportunity for more people. And most important is that they help us feel proud of who we are and where we are from.

Recast Your City and Value It

What do I mean by saying that the people and the place feel valued? It means that people feel that they are a part of a community.

Are you proud to say that you're from your hometown or neighborhood? Do you feel connected to your neighbors and local business owners? Do you feel like you are part of that place? Do you walk along main street or downtown and think, yes, this is part of who I am, this is where I belong? Then you probably feel valued in your community. You feel like you are a part of it, like you are included.

Does the place feel valued? Here, value is a tougher concept to define. It might mean that the storefronts are filled and in good repair. It might mean that neighbors have businesses along the block and sweep the sidewalk out front daily. It might mean that the corner store is owned by someone who knows your name or that you can stroll down the street and say hello to the business owners you know. It might be something as simple (or not so simple) as people from all different backgrounds feeling connected and included in the downtown.

It also might mean that the local government invests in the place. Does the city (or county) spend money repairing and improving the sidewalks? Does the government sponsor programming along main street where people can come together for celebrations? Signs that a place is valued can be as mundane as good lighting, narrow car lanes that slow traffic and make people feel safer, or storefronts that are painted and clean through support from the city.

All these pieces come together to help us feel connected to the community (be it the neighborhood, town, or city) where we are valued and where that place is valued and feels worthy of investment from us. How it is valued—and what that means—should be up to the people who live there.

We know what a place looks like when it is not valued. Buildings sit empty. Main Street is struggling. People see other places thriving but feel like it's just not possible for them. Downtown is a place only for tourists or other visitors, but not for the locals. Or perhaps Main Street only reflects part of the community and not its demographic diversity, so many local residents don't feel like they belong. Neighbors may feel like they are completely on their own if they want to start a business, and many people are left out of local economic opportunities. The place might be full but missing energy (storefronts with blinds down because the stores are really filled with offices), or it might be blocks of buildings owned by people who live far away and just let the buildings sit empty and fall apart.

To save downtown, we need to commit to value both the people and the place. And small-scale manufacturing businesses are a way to get there.

Why Now?

Local leaders have been doing some things right for our communities over the last few decades and some things very wrong. Recent events made it glaringly clear just how bad it has gotten, if you didn't see it before. And it's time—beyond time—for us to do better.

Inclusive economic prosperity means that everyone has the opportunity to contribute to and benefit from the ability to build wealth. It means that people who were historically excluded from wealth building, specifically Black residents and other people of color, have as much ability to participate in these successes as anyone else in the community.[3]

Although there are many people and organizations working on economic development, place-based economic development, placemaking, revitalization, and many other concepts with wonky terms for investing in people and places, the reality is that most people in most places have been investing in a way that increases the racial wealth gap and upholds the systemic racism from our past economic development and planning decisions.

On top of that, COVID-19 hit in 2020, and hundreds of thousands of lives and livelihoods across the United States were lost. The vast majority of US businesses closed completely for two to three months due to shelter-in-place requirements, and most can only partially reopen until the crisis is over. More than forty million people filed for unemployment starting in March 2020.[4] The US economy shrank by 9.5 percent in the second quarter of 2020, the largest drop in modern record.[5] We also saw that the impact on lives lost and businesses closed was much greater in the Black community than in the White one.[6]

We need to do better—for our communities and for the people in our communities. And now is the time to make a commitment to build our local economies in a different way and take a new path forward. Now is the time to say that we are ready to truly strengthen our local economy, build wealth opportunities for more people, and create thriving downtowns that bring our neighbors together. To get there, though, we will need to do a lot of things differently.

Even before the COVID-19 crisis, the United States was facing a stark economic reality at both the national and local levels that set us up for the extreme economic impacts of the pandemic. Consider the following details from before the shutdown:

⚙ Eighty percent of all counties were already seeing a decline in their working-age adult population.[7] That statistic means that the vast majority of places were losing people, losing expertise, and, for many, losing hope. What does that look like at the local level? It's the brain drain that many rural and tourism-centric towns talk about: their youth graduate from high school and leave the area to find better employment. Anyone who can get out does get out. It's true of many legacy cities as well. For example, in Youngstown, Ohio, a young adult told me that she needed to get permission from her mother to move back to town for work because her mother expected and wanted her to move elsewhere for better opportunities.

⚙ Income inequality was at the highest it had ever been since the US Census Bureau began reporting it.[8] The United States became a country of haves and have-nots. It became a country of extremes. Never before have so many people made so little money and so few made so much. For instance, in 1967, the Census Bureau found that the top 5 percent of earners in the United States earned a median of about $185,300, whereas the lowest 20 percent earned just over $10,500; in 2018, those numbers went to $416,500 and $13,700, respectively.[9] In that time span, the top 5 percent of earners increased their income by more than 300 percent, whereas the lowest 20 percent of earners increased their income by only 30 percent. And those are the medians in each of those groups, not the full range of incomes.

⚙ Vacant storefronts in thousands of cities and towns depressed property values and investment by 20 percent or more.[10] Many places lost their downtown economy when major businesses moved their production to other countries in the 1970s and 1980s or moved jobs out to the suburbs. Others lost it when their zoning and economic development groups pushed for malls and big-box retail near highways in the 1980s and 1990s. Independent retailers have closed at astonishing rates since the 1980s, when they supplied about half of the country's sales needs, to now, when they cover only a fourth of those sales.[11] Neighborhood and town center storefronts emptied out all over the United States. In addition, many places never recovered from the 2008 Great Recession and the more recent transition to online sales. Vacant storefronts contribute to a vicious cycle, because vacancy depresses the values of other nearby properties and pushes people away from the area, thereby reducing value and interest even more.

These economic indicators show a country divided and unequal. When we dig a little deeper, we can see that the divides are along racial and ethnic lines, along income disparities, and across urban-rural lines. Yet we continue to use the very same strategies in local economic development that created these inequities, that dug us deeper into these inequities, even though we know that we are in a completely different era with different needs and different values.

We need to take a clear-eyed look at where we've been and stop hiding from it. Then we need to take an honest look at what's worked, who it's worked for, and who it hasn't worked for. Then we can change our course and invest in the actions that make the biggest difference for the most people and build a new, stronger, more inclusive economy for our communities.

If you agree with these goals, keep reading. If you believe in building community pride, participation, and ownership in an inclusive way, keep reading. If not, this book isn't for you.

In this book, you will read about where we went wrong in economic development and downtown investment, how to create a better path to reach your goals, and how to employ a new method to get there. You will learn how to bring small-scale manufacturing into the conversation to help save your downtown, your neighborhood, or your village center—you pick.

Recast Your City is a how-to book. No wonky stuff (or at least only a little), just clear explanations and steps, with online worksheets available at www.RecastYourCity.com, to help you make changes in your community.

Are you ready to dive into how to make this change happen, help your hometown or neighborhood be a valued place, and make sure that the people in your community, especially small-business owners, feel valued?

Consider this the start of our conversation.

Throughout this book, I often refer to "us" or "we." That's because this book is a conversation. It is a conversation that you and I will start here to make our cities, towns, and neighborhoods stronger places with more opportunity for more people, no matter where we live.

Why Should You Keep Reading?

The *Oxford English Dictionary* tells us that "recast" means to "give (a metal object) a different form by melting it down and reshaping it." *Recast Your City* is a way to give new shape to your local economy and bring energy to your downtown. It will help you create the opportunity to bring people together to believe in their community again.

This book is all about bringing main streets, downtowns, and old neighborhood centers back to life. It is about creating a place filled with businesses that represent the demographic diversity of the community. It is about creating a brand new downtown (for those still missing one) that showcases all that is amazing about that place. It is about true economic development success—a model that includes everyone, not just a few.

This book is for you if you are a local government leader who believes in your community, not just in listening to some of the people in your community.

This book is for you if you are a local leader in real estate and you want to create a place that holds its value for a long, long time because there is no other place like it.

This book is for you if you lead a nonprofit organization that works with small businesses and entrepreneurs and you are ready to rally your community to partner with these businesses and help them grow.

This book is for you if you manage a downtown, main street, business improvement district, land bank, or community development corporation and you are ready for some new ideas to bring your community into the limelight and make it a thriving place that benefits everyone.

This book is for you if you believe in your community, you believe in all that it can be, and you are done waiting for the cavalry to come and save your town. It is for you if you are ready to get your hands dirty and help make it happen.

Tina Shelvin in the McComb-Veazey neighborhood and business owners like Katie Stack of Stitch & Rivet are community leaders who know that everyone deserves to feel like they are part of their community and to live in a place that feels valued. They see that small-scale manufacturing businesses can help them rebuild that value and pride in the community.

Too many local efforts focus only on big, long-term plans. They are important, and there is a place for them. But we sometimes forget that we still need to act in the short-term—the here and now—to build toward those larger changes. Recasting your city is not just about the celebratory ribbon-cutting events, but rather the little things that all build to it. This book will give you the tools to make changes now, with new actions that can be implemented in three to nine months.

This book gives you the method to figure out what those immediate actions need to be so that you can achieve your long-term goals. It helps you create a map to implement changes that will be most effective to build a strong, resilient, and growing community of small businesses, including small-scale manufacturing.

If you are ready to act now, if you are impatient to make things better in your community, if you are done sitting and waiting for the big idea to fix everything at once, this book is for you. If you follow all the steps in this book and use the online tools, you will have some immediate wins, which will help people in the community feel valued now and inspired to work on the larger, harder pieces with you.

Why Listen to Me?

But why should you listen to me? Blame it on my parents. My mother was a school nurse for more than twenty years, and she taught me a lot of things. One lesson that has stayed with me was that every child should feel valued and loved. She also said that every child—every one of them—should know that they are valuable and worthy of that love.

She also taught me how to hang blinds, measuring three times to get it right, and how to use a drill to finish the project. She sewed, painted, quilted, and crocheted and just thought of those skills as things she worked on. She wasn't a "creative" and she didn't sell what she made, yet she always enjoyed learning how to do those things just a little bit better. When I was a kid, her wild and crazy idea was to open a shop with one of her friends. She never did open the shop, but her belief in people, and her passion for making things, shaped who I am today.

My father, on the other hand, can't hang blinds, but he taught me to love places. He showed me the love of wandering downtown streets, meeting all different people, and feeling at home in big and small cities. An immigrant to the United States when he was seven years old, my father was the beneficiary of a public school education at a science magnet program that changed his trajectory. He received a free college education not because of a competitive scholarship, but because the local city college was free. After getting his PhD, he fought for environmental protections, teaching me that we need to do good in the world, especially for people who may not have a seat at the table.

As a result of my parents' influences, I became a city planner. I focused on all the pieces of how to make a great place. I worked on housing policy, transportation policy, and all the local politics of getting people to invest in downtowns—before so many people moved back downtown.

I worked with large and small cities all over the United States. I led the technical assistance program at the US Environmental Protection

Agency's Smart Growth Program and served as vice president and chief of staff at the national nonprofit organization Smart Growth America.

Somewhere along the way, I realized that housing and transportation policy, city streets, and building design just weren't enough. They were essential ingredients, but without people believing in their community, without leadership who believed in that place, and without an inclusive table to make those decisions, creating a "great place" meant creating it for just some of the people there. It certainly didn't give us a way to create a strong local economy.

So I started to look at local businesses. What kind of small business made the biggest difference in a neighborhood? What kind of business created multiple benefits, not just jobs, that could help bring a downtown back to life?

I worked with many cities and towns to talk about "more jobs" or the "jobs-housing balance" as a goal. We talked about how to bring jobs back downtown. I worked on policies and real estate models to encourage both housing and jobs on Main Street. But then I realized that we missed a step in this work.

We never asked the tough questions:

What kind of jobs do we want? Are they offering a living wage?

Which businesses get to be downtown? Who owns those businesses?

Who is downtown for? Who gets to participate in downtown?

Who should benefit and build wealth from the investments in downtown or a main street?

Are there different answers when we work on downtown versus an older neighborhood main street?

Do different kinds of businesses make a bigger difference in a downtown than others?

Is the answer to that last question dependent on our goals?

We always talked policy, but we never talked about the goals of the people who live there. We never talked about how different community goals might change the type of development and investment necessary in downtown or a neighborhood main street.

I'm not talking about goals with names like "improve placemaking" that mean different things to each person. The concept might be important, but that language is not how people live or experience a place. Instead, I'm talking about these goals:

Increase opportunities for more residents to build wealth through entrepreneurship on main street.

Ensure that our downtown storefront tenants are unique so that we stand out from all the neighboring towns (and hold value over time).

Focus economic development spending to increase the number of living wage jobs.

Create new real estate models that help more local business owners thrive and stay in town.

I then started talking to people about how these kinds of goals affect the way we redevelop and reinvest in downtown, main street, or a neighborhood center and how we achieve the wanted outcomes. After much research and experience, I concluded that small-scale manufacturing businesses are the essential ingredient to help us achieving those goals. So, after eighteen years in the federal government, nonprofit, and private sectors, I combined my love of places and locals who love those places with my belief in the value of every place and every person. Impatient to make things happen now in communities, in 2014 I launched Recast City, which partners with local leaders to bring main street back to life, bring business back to downtown, and build an inclusive and resilient economy with small-scale manufacturing businesses.

Honestly, my lifelong passion is to help people make great places by bringing the hidden gem of small-scale product businesses into today's mixed-use development, commercial property repositioning, and local economic development strategy. Consider listening to me because of my experience, my belief in the greatness of your community, or my passion to help you make it happen. But really, listen to the examples in this book that come from the many communities that have used this method, created their own immediate wins, and are now building their big successes.

From Columbia, Missouri, to Knoxville, Tennessee, and from Fremont, California, to Hoboken, New Jersey, this method of recasting a city has helped local leaders understand their small-business community, their local economic development, and the needs of their downtown. These leaders understand the barriers to new development and the rehabilitation of storefronts. They now know local small-scale manufacturing businesses and understand how these business owners can be catalysts to achieve their community goals. These leaders started to implement (within a month!) immediate steps to make a difference now and create a great place with thriving businesses.

Recast City and this book are a culmination of my years as a city planner in community redevelopment providing technical assistance to cities and towns all over the United States. My passion is figuring out the puzzle of making great places, ones that reflect the personality and the needs of that specific place and the people in that community—and nowhere else.

Recast Your City is my way of sharing all the lessons I've learned along the way, all the details about how to work with communities differently, and all the steps you need to build a stronger, more inclusive, and more resilient downtown and local economy.

Map of the Book

The next chapter of this book covers how we've been doing economic development in a way that leaves most people and places behind and how some of the pieces that have been missing from our economic development work can make a big difference to help more people and more places be stronger. Chapter 3 then defines a new path forward in economic development to create thriving places with thriving local businesses that includes small-scale manufacturing businesses and an inclusive community of business owners.

Chapter 4 introduces Recast City's five-step method to save your downtown with small-scale manufacturing. This section introduces you to all the pieces that we get into detail about in the rest of the chapters.

Chapter 5 helps you understand the lay of the land in your community, key assets, and outcomes you want to achieve in this work. These steps might be something you've done before, but not in this way. Here, we'll go through a series of questions focusing on eight different elements that you need to think through at the start. We only make change happen when we know who should benefit and in what way.

In chapter 6, we work through how to find and connect with key people for this work. Methods to find small-scale manufacturing business owners, property owners, and essential Connectors in your community to ensure that your work includes the diversity of your community for maximum impact are included in this chapter.

Chapter 7 introduces user research and discusses how we use this technique for interviews with business owners, property owners, and other key people who need to be brought in at the start of the work.

In this chapter, you will get background on user research in general, as well as detailed steps and draft questionnaires to use in your interviews.

In chapter 8, we work together to analyze what you hear from all your interviews. Our analysis will follow those eight key elements for successful economic and real estate development, which includes small-scale manufacturing in downtown. In this chapter, the places that successfully implemented the Recast City method and followed through on their actions are discussed, and we talk about how you will get there, too. You will understand how other cities—from Grants Pass, Oregon, to Cincinnati, Ohio—have made this method work so that you can make changes in your community right now.

The final chapter, chapter 9, is all about getting started and making it happen. Remember that this book is all about taking action, and this chapter launches you into this work.

You can access tools, worksheets, and templates at www.RecastYourCity. com. Print them, write on them, and make other people write on them. The method works best if you use all the worksheets and really push yourself to think hard about different questions with different people.

Before You Get Started

I want to thank you for believing in your community, for caring about everyone in your city or town and not just some of the people, for believing in your community's greatness, and for your impatience to see it happen now. The Recast City method is your first step. Although it takes a lot of work, this method works, and it makes an enormous difference— both immediately and long term. Local leaders who used this method launched commercial shared kitchens, started coworking spaces for small manufacturing, and brought small producers into new and redeveloped real estate projects. They brought excitement and energy to long-forgotten corridors of the city and to small-town main streets that had seen better days. To grow their economy in new ways, they created new business development programs specific to this sector and reached business owners whom they had never spoken to before. They created jobs, helped more businesses launch, and strengthened their local economy.

The benefits of this work come to your community, your small businesses, and your downtown, but they also come to you. This method helps each person see the talents of their neighbors, the goodwill between business owners, and the belief in your amazing place full of potential.

Let's get started!

The Old Economic Model Left People and Places Behind

CHAPTER 2

Why We Need a New Economic Development Model

THE ECONOMIC DEVELOPMENT MODEL most local governments use today created a reality of the haves and have nots. A few people in a few places are winning in the economy, with more jobs, more investment, and more wealth. Everyone else is losing—or working really hard to tread water.

The old model is dependent on tax incentives and benefits for a small portion of our population. Today, we need a new economic development model that can support both urban and rural places; that supports people across economic, racial, and ethnic lines; and that gets major investment and support from local and state leaders.

We need a new model that helps us save our downtowns and build strong local economies that include everyone.

Before we can pick a new path forward, however, it is essential to understand what didn't work in the old model and why the mistakes we made created such an environment of winners and losers.

Most of the economic development strategies used today in local government are left over from the 1970s. These strategies were used when the United States had an economy dominated by rapid employment growth, racially motivated White flight from urban centers to the outlying suburbs, and racial discrimination in economic and real estate development decision-making. They are strategies from before the internet, before the Affordable Care Act, before venture capital and impact investing, and certainly from before COVID-19 and Black Lives Matter. They are relics from another era.

In 1970, a new house cost less than $24,000, the national average income was just under $10,000, and a gallon of gasoline cost $0.36.[1] Ponchos, bell-bottoms, and disco were all the rage in the 1970s. *Saturday Night Live* went live for the first time, Walt Disney World's main street opened in Florida, the first Boeing 747 took flight, and Apple II was released to the public from an unknown little company. The three largest businesses in the United States were General Motors, Exxon, and the Ford Motor Company. US Steel and Bethlehem Steel were in the top twenty-five grossing companies.[2] There was major job growth, but it was also the decade when the number of people in white-collar jobs first overtook the number of people in blue-collar jobs.[3] In many places, manufacturing jobs were still the main employer, but the role of manufacturing was slipping, and these jobs would drop in major numbers over the next three decades.

In 1970, US population was just over 200 million people,[4] 82 percent of the national workforce was White–not Hispanic, 11 percent of the workforce was Black, and 43 percent of women were in the labor force. In 1972, only 190,000 businesses were Black-owned (2 percent of all the businesses in the United States), 120,000 businesses were owned by Latino people (1 percent),[5] and just over 400,000 businesses were owned by women (5 percent).[6] The five largest cities were mostly in the North: New York City, Chicago, Los Angeles, Philadelphia, and Detroit.[7] The 1970s also saw the end of the sixty years of the Great Migration, when six million Black people moved from the South to northern and western cities for better opportunities.

The decade also left us with burnt-out neighborhoods from the riots in the 1960s, a legacy of redlining that only allowed Black families to move into specific neighborhoods or prevented them from getting mortgages (even though that was illegal by then), and discrimination against women, including losing jobs because they were pregnant.[8] There was rampant inflation and an oil embargo, with people waiting hours to fill their cars' gas tanks.

It was an economy in which many citizens—particularly Black people and women—were still fighting for an entry point into the economy. The Civil Rights Act passed in 1964, but discrimination against Black employees was alive and strong. Economic independence for women was also a very new fight.

Today, the population of the United States is more than 330 million people.[9] Before COVID-19 hit, the US labor force had 57 percent of women and 69 percent of men working in it.[10] Looking at the total US population today, 60 percent of the population is White only, and twenty-one of the twenty-five largest counties have populations that are majority people of color.[11] In 2012, there were 2.6 million Black-owned businesses (9 percent) and 3.3 million Latino-owned businesses (12 percent) out of a total 27.6 million businesses in the United States.[12] In 2019, women-owned businesses represented 42 percent of all businesses, and women of color accounted for half of all the women-owned businesses. The number of Black women-owned businesses grew by 50 percent from 2014 to 2019.[13] In the United States, the median price of a new house is now $250,000,[14] the national median income is about $62,000,[15] and a gallon of gas cost $2.10.[16]

Our dominant jobs today are in the service, retail, and hospitality industries, with workers earning low-wages, and not in blue-collar, middle-income jobs.[17] Housing affordability is a major challenge in many large markets, and the investment in downtowns exploded in some places. Climate change is creating real estate pressure to move to higher ground, often displacing people already in those places, and the nation faces growing wealth disparities based on race, income, and location.

Businesses people couldn't dream of in the 1970s are now worth billions of dollars. Companies like Airbnb and WeWork changed the way people vacation and where they work. Twitter, Facebook, Instagram, and Snapchat changed the way people communicate. Tesla, Uber, and Lyft showed us that there are different ways to get around. People operate businesses off computers, tablets, and smartphones through the internet that didn't exist in the 1970s. The majority of people now get their daily news off social media, platforms we couldn't imagine back then.

Black Lives Matter has become the largest movement in US history, with more than fifteen million people joining in protests,[18] and COVID-19 threw everyone's lives and economy in the air. Black and Brown members of our communities died from the pandemic at twice the rate as White members.[19] The economy, and the people in it, changed.

Our lives in 2020 do not look like 1970. And our demographic, cultural, and economic differences only amplify our need to pursue economic development in a different way.

Much has been written on economic disparities and the systemic racism in economic development and land use decisions that caused many of these disparities.[20] White flight, discriminatory practices that pulled money and support from the cities, and incentives to move retail out of cities and to places off highway exit ramps all illustrate the abandonment of the people and the places in our cities over decades.

In some places today, some of those development and land use decisions are getting changed, and it's a good start.

But we continue to make mistakes. Let's talk about those first.

Three Critical Mistakes

Three mistakes—chasing big business, restricting economic development to the same historic winners, and emphasizing new real estate development over all else—need to be understood and overcome. Only then can we build great places with thriving businesses and a resilient and inclusive local economy.

Mistake 1: Chase Big Business at All Costs

Because they need to compete with their neighbors for tax revenue, local governments are convinced that big business is king. This means that many jurisdictions spend local dollars hunting for the next big game to steal (I mean recruit) from somewhere else. They compete for a big business in hopes of bringing in jobs and new tax revenue that will have a trickle-down effect on the rest of the local economy. Some economic development leaders spend millions of public dollars to recruit businesses that promise a hundred jobs. Everyone gets a shiny ribbon cutting and a picture with their big-game win.

This model creates problems, however. One is based on trickle-down economics, and another is based on the types of jobs offered.

1 *Local government spends millions or even billions of dollars on recruitment that is based on trickle-down economic benefits that rarely achieve the goals of the community.* The recruitment money offered by local government usually comes in the form of property tax or income tax breaks, building new roads and water infrastructure to support the business, or constructing new business parks on speculation so that the community has "move-in ready" sites. In return, the business promises how many jobs it will bring to the community and how long those jobs will stay. The business offers projections of how much tax revenues will go up because its employees spend locally.

A high-profile example of this practice is the national competition for Amazon's second headquarters, HQ2. In 2018, nearly five hundred jurisdictions submitted applications to woo Amazon's second headquarters into their community. With a promise of twenty-five thousand jobs, it was recruitment at a different scale. Amazon was offered local and state incentives totaling nearly $3 billion to locate in Long Island City, Queens. Amazon chose New York as a site, but eventually pulled out of the deal due to backlash at the level of incentives offered. Residents and many local leaders questioned whether this arrangement would be the best use of $3 billion in investment. The Association for Housing and Neighborhood Development said that the deal "not only disempowers the very communities that will be most impacted, but entirely erases their agency and their voices."[21] Adding to the friction is that these decisions are often made behind closed doors, with no transparency and few metrics.

Unfortunately, most recruitment dollars do not recoup the investment; instead, a jurisdiction just pays a business for the decision it was likely to make anyway.[22] When the local economic development leaders trade away future tax benefits through a recruitment package, the community gives up ten to twenty years of property tax or other benefits from that business. In some states, that discounted tax rate remains in perpetuity. In addition, if the business's employees commute from a nearby town and spend their money there, the spillover effects on local retail spending are little to nothing. Often, after the tax break period is over, the big business threatens to leave the jurisdiction and renegotiates a longer tax break or other expensive benefits to bribe it to stay—or the business simply leaves town.

Research from Good Jobs First shows that the biggest deals pay extreme dollars—up to $456,000 per job—to recruit a large business from somewhere nearby or across state lines.[23] Think about that for a moment—that's nearly a half million dollars *per job*. It means that the local government decided that jobs from outside of the community, jobs that could leave in the future, are more important (by a number of magnitudes) than any job currently in the community or any job that could be created in the community. It means that local leaders decided that instead of funding a variety of economic development projects (for instance, helping more local businesses launch, grow, and create the same number of jobs that are less likely to leave the community), all this funding goes to support one business.

In 1978, Pennsylvania invested more than $90 million to lure a Volkswagen Rabbit manufacturing plant to the western part of the state with tax breaks. The state built a new rail spur, rehabbed an old automaker complex, and leased it to VW on the cheap. Ten years later, VW decided to stop producing the Rabbit and closed the plant; as a result, five thousand people lost their jobs. At the time, Pennsylvania Governor Milton Shapp said, "We did get 10 years out of it, so you can't call it a total loss."[24] But the question really is, what is the trade-off? If the state had instead spent $90 million in that region teaching people to be entrepreneurs and growing locally owned businesses, would the region not have fallen off a cliff of job loss and instead built a more sustainable local economy?

2 *Most recruitment incentives focus on the extremes, not middle-income jobs.* Many states and local jurisdictions have tax abatement deals for companies and little to no oversight regarding job creation and benefits to the local economy.[25] Some economic development authorities have grant-funding incentives to recruit businesses with only a significant number of high-paying jobs or to recruit a warehouse or distribution center with low-wage jobs. Rarely is funding available at the same scale for business types with more middle-income jobs.

For instance, the Economic Development Fund Grant and Loan Program in Montgomery County, Maryland, will provide a grant to recruit or retain a growing business. Applicants for the fund are evaluated using an economic impact analysis that weighs the number of jobs and the salaries of those jobs. The analysis often gives a higher priority to projects that commit to more high-paying jobs over middle-income ones.[26] On the one hand, it is great that the county runs an economic impact analysis on these decisions. On the other hand, it is a county with as many households earning more than $200,000 as earn less than $50,000 in an expensive market. A focus on strong middle-income jobs could make a bigger long-term difference in a county whose population is diverse (56 percent of the population is Black, Latino, and Asian) but where Black and Latino households are twice as more likely than other households to make less than $50,000.[27]

When high-income jobs are the focus, communities recruit businesses with jobs that many of the local residents are not trained for or qualified to fill. Some of those high-paying jobs are therefore likely to be filled by people who commute from somewhere else in the region and may never benefit the local community. It means that the community increasingly has only high-paying jobs in the recruited business and low-paying jobs for the services they need, but nothing in the middle. When we don't invest in good-paying middle-income jobs, we don't get them.

In other cases, states and localities provide tax break incentives for warehousing and distribution centers to supposedly bring jobs to the community but end up giving away millions of dollars for jobs that are barely above minimum wage. Amazon distribution centers in Ohio received more than $123 million from the state, while more than 10 percent of that workforce (many of whom were part-time employees) qualified for food stamps. Over time, the incentives cost much more than just the tax breaks.[28]

In addition, on average less than 10 to 30 percent of these new jobs go to state or local residents who are not already employed. In many cases, the new jobs go to people whom the large business brings into the community.[29] The deals often just shuffle people around and don't create new opportunities for local residents who are unemployed or underemployed. In general, about 75 percent of the time, these incentives don't even influence a business's decision about where to locate.

A few organizations question this kind of recruitment spending, but it rarely makes big press (unless it's the Amazon competition for HQ2). Yet time and time again, these recruitment giveaways fall short of recouping their investment and often redirect money that could be invested in local businesses. What benefits could our local businesses create if they received comparable support?

Economic leaders wave numbers around about direct and indirect impacts when they talk about how a big business will create four more local jobs in the community for each one created by the recruited business. No one, however, talks about the types of jobs that will be created.

In some communities, there may be a time and a place for some recruitment spending, but the questions of who benefits and what is trying to be achieved with this spending need to be examined. If we want to create an inclusive and resilient local economy (you can't get one without the other), we need to think about how we invest in all kinds of living-wage jobs, opportunities for diverse households to build wealth, and what kinds of actions get us there.

Mistake 2: Economic Development
Is Only for Some People in Some Places

We can see that money only flows to some people in some places through investment decisions by local governments (especially around land use), venture capitalists, and banks. This reality means that our economic system is leaving many communities behind while a few communities thrive. And the distance between these two groups is widening fast.

In Lafayette, Louisiana, for example, local government investment to fix up a neighborhood main street goes to the predominantly wealthy, White neighborhood to the south of downtown, not to the lower-income Black and Creole neighborhood main street in need of repaved roads, safe sidewalks, and a grocery store. Some cities invest even farther away from the historic downtown; one example is Newport, Washington, which invested in a new business park on spec at the edge of town instead of in its historic main street.

This same phenomenon was seen in the response to small-business needs during the COVID-19 shutdown. Because first come, first served was the basis of most loan and grant programs, those who had the resources were able to navigate the complicated process and get in line early, with no regard to who needed the support the most to stay in business.

The gap is widening between the have and have-not places. Between 2005 and 2017, five metropolitan areas (Boston, San Francisco, San Jose, Seattle, and San Diego) accounted for 90 percent of all innovation job growth. By 2017, more than two-thirds of all venture capital investment went to businesses in five metropolitan areas (San Francisco, New York City, San Jose, Boston, and Los Angeles).[30]

Businesses throughout the United States—especially outside of the largest cities—struggle to get access to private-sector investment and do not get the attention of their local governments. These businesses can create better-paying jobs and increase local employment on main street, but they are not the priority for investment. The private sector in charge of the capital consistently shows a bias toward the largest cities. The system of investing in a few businesses in a few places is self-reinforcing.

There are some efforts to redirect some of this investment; one is Steve Case's Rise of the Rest Seed Fund, which is putting $300 million into businesses with high growth potential that are located outside of the major cities. A few local governments are also starting to focus investment dollars on locally owned businesses. In most cases, however, decisions about where and how to invest are just widening the gap and leaving more people and places behind.

Two additional factors—Opportunity Zones and the racial wealth gap—also contribute to this economic discrepancy.

1 *Opportunity Zones didn't help.* Opportunity Zones are part of a tax incentive to change investment behavior that came with changes in the 2017 Tax Cuts and Jobs Act. When the Opportunity Zones program was launched, every jurisdiction had the chance to define geographic areas for new investment. This program created a way for wealthy individuals or corporations to invest their capital gains into designated areas to encourage investment in places in need. The investors would pay little to no tax on the capital gains if they invested in real estate or businesses in those locations for a specific amount of time.

   The places getting the investments and the real estate projects, however, are those that were in the pipeline in 2017 when these zones were created. The investments went to places where the returns would be strong anyway, with a target of a 15 to 18 percent return on investment on top of the tax break. No one said, "I can get a great tax break on the investment, so I'll expect less of a return out of the project itself." The major tax benefit did not change the calculation of real estate investment; it only accelerated the process. The zones created a greater push between cities and towns, with even more haves and have-nots across the country.

All research on Opportunity Zones is self-reported; the Internal Revenue Service does not require that participating funds disclose the investment details. By April 2020, just over $10 billion in investment was reported, with 97 percent of the investment going to real estate projects.[31] Because investors are looking for the highest return possible in the ten-year requirement, most of the investment is going to the major cities. The investments seem to be very relationship based: people who know the high-wealth individuals who earned all that money from the stock market and other investments (capital gains) could approach them to invest in big projects already on the move in those big cities. Very little investment is reported going into local businesses and job creation in the Opportunity Zones, even though support for small businesses was a big selling point of the program.[32] And there is no report of any investment directed to support Black business owners, who might be the dominant business owners in an Opportunity Zone.

2 *The racial wealth gap keeps getting bigger.* The old economic development model did not address inequities in the United States, but in fact made many of them worse, especially across racial lines that were very clear in the 1970s and are still clear today.

In 2019, the greatest income inequity in the United States ever recorded was reported.[33] The nation also has a major racial wealth gap. White households have about six-and-a-half times the wealth of Black households.[34] This gap is due to historical injustices (such as redlining, which kept Black families from building wealth through home ownership, and discriminatory employment practices that relegated Black employees to lower-paying jobs) and continued unequal incomes. As reported in 2019, research by the Federal Reserve Bank of Cleveland showed that the racial wealth gap has barely changed since before the passage of the Civil Rights Act of 1964, and without purposeful change, the racial wealth gap will take more than 250 years to close.[35] If incomes are matched, however, the gap could be closed in two generations. Yes, that's still a really long time, but by only investing in jobs for some people and not addressing this income gap, we continue to build a weak and divided economy.

This gap persists at every education level. On average, Black people with advanced degrees earn 82 percent of what their White counterparts earn, and those with college degrees earn 76 percent of what their White counterparts earn.[36] Even at the lowest national unemployment rate, right before the pandemic hit, Black people had double the unemployment rate of White people. In 1968, the Black median income was 55 percent of what White workers earned.[37] In 2016, Black people earned 65 percent of what White people earned on average.[38] That is forty-eight years with only a 10 percent change. And COVID-19 shutdowns only made it worse.

In May 2020, in the middle of the COVID shutdown, only 50 percent of Black men and 47 percent of Black women were employed.[39] Seventeen percent of frontline workers were from communities of color.[40] In addition, Black-owned businesses were overwhelmingly in sectors hit hard by the shutdowns, especially in service businesses and health care assistance. These businesses had to close completely for an extended period, often with little savings to support the family and little grant support from federal, state, and local small-business programs. While 20 percent of all businesses closed from February to May 2020, that number was 40 percent of Black-owned businesses. That is, 450,000 business owners closed for months.[41]

Given these challenges, how do we change the way we invest in our communities to make every person, every business, and every neighborhood center stronger? What is the role of our local investment dollars? Every dollar we spend in economic development, every zoning decision we make, every rehabilitated building or new construction we approve is an investment decision for our community.

If venture capital only focuses on a few places, what is the role of local government dollars? Who should benefit from them? Can our local economies grow faster and stronger by closing the racial wealth gap? If so, how can we do that? How do we help more people of color have higher-income jobs? And what investments help us get there? (We will start answering these questions in chapter 4.)

Mistake 3: New Real Estate Development Is Always the Goal

The third major mistake is that we often build new real estate without thinking about the best end goals for the community. Local governments want investment, so they will sometimes take any kind of new development that is proposed. Places that are struggling often don't think about who the project will benefit, how it will help achieve broad community goals, and how it will help build a stronger economy in the longer term.

The way real estate development operates today is not necessarily community minded. Real estate is a commodity. Single-family homes are part of national and international investment portfolios. Major institutions, private equity funds, hedge funds, pension funds, and real estate investment trusts invest in real estate to earn income.[42]

Investors are generally looking for short-term returns within five to seven years. For the national investment companies that own thousands of single-family rental homes, achieving that goal means cutting costs, limiting repairs, and letting properties decline. In downtowns, it often means leaving main street buildings empty to take the tax credit from the loss of revenue and leaving that downtown to decline. In new construction, it often means building an inexpensive, boring building that doesn't contribute to the place and actually takes away from the character of the place. It is almost saying that this place is not worthy of a building that reflects its true value. In all cases, it means limiting local ownership of downtown and wealth-building opportunities for residents, as the problems created by commodity investors get amplified by local government policies that create more inequity in more places and for more people.

Three additional aspects of real estate decision-making—outdated outreach methods, an oversupply of retail space, and inconsistent approval processes—stand out as mistakes we need to fix to make more great places for the people who live there.

1 *Our outreach methods for community engagement are outdated
   and set us up for failure.* We all know what passes for outreach in
   a lot of places: the public agency hosts a public meeting at the
   public building, and a notification inviting the public goes into
   the local newspaper or on the city's website. This model assumes
   that everyone potentially affected by that project has the ability
   to drop whatever they do in life, travel to that public building,
   and spend hours sitting through that event. The reality of this
   outreach method is that it doesn't reach new voices and doesn't
   find new ideas. In most communities, the same few people tend
   to show up each meeting. Getting input only from this kind of
   public meeting limits the voices of the vast majority (if not nearly
   all) of the people who will be affected by the decisions.

   Outreach is often done to obtain feedback only after a project
   has been planned. The ideas and solutions are originally generated by the local government or developer, not by the community
   being impacted.[43] The process is transactional, not necessarily
   inclusive; limits contact to those already with the most influence; and creates relationships that are only short term and will

not help change anything in the community over the long term. This old method means that any solution most likely does not sufficiently take the needs of the community into account, that relationships are not built for the long term, and that the leaders of the process aren't open to discovering new assets and new ideas generated by the community.

Examples of this failure can be seen across the United States, from big city to small town. In the end, policies are passed and programs are adopted that don't meet the needs of the target population—and in some cases harm them. We get wasteful projects where people wonder why that program did not work or if people just didn't need the help. In reality, however, the program was not shaped with direct input from the people who needed it.

Think about it. Think about the investments in neighborhoods that end up displacing neighborhood residents because the investments were not geared for the people living there now, there is no opportunity for community ownership, and the projects are focused on people being recruited to the area (even if that wasn't the initial intention). They are a result of who was involved in the process, who created the ideas, and who developed the solutions.

2 *We spread retail everywhere, like expensive peanut butter, and over-supply the market.* We once plopped indoor retail malls all over the United States. Then, when real estate developers realized that investing in downtowns again was worthwhile, we built a lot of vertical mixed-use projects with retail on the ground floor and offices or apartments above it. As a result, by 2018, the United States had the most retail space per capita of any country in the world. It even had 50 percent more space per capita than its closest neighbor in retail space and geography, Canada.[44]

State and local governments chase retail space because so many budgets are dependent on sales tax. States that have sales tax depend on it for anywhere from 15 to 46 percent of the total state budget. Local governments collected more than $100 billion in sales tax in 2016, contributing to about 11 percent of total local revenues.[45] But the localities also get more than 30 percent of their local budget from the state. So if sales taxes are lower for the state, the impact of sales tax collection hits each local budget from multiple sides.

Today, the reality of retail is changing. From 2017 to 2019, many large-format retailers started to close stores and shrink their footprints. Major national businesses, including GAP, Abercrombie & Fitch, Gymboree, Family Dollar, and JC Penney, closed dozens to hundreds of stores. More than eight thousand major chain retail stores closed in 2017, and another five thousand closed in 2019,[46] with these chains retaining only their high-traffic "prime location" stores.

Then COVID-19 shut down everything. For three months in the spring of 2020, all retail stores closed in many states. After that, many places allowed stores to only open at 50 percent of their capacity. Many people worried about the health impacts of in-person shopping and minimizing their outings. The immediate future is expected to be unpredictable and full of business openings and closings. Consumer fears and lack of confidence in their financial security also make the in-person retail outlook look bleak.

By contrast, the rate of growth in retail space was astonishing in the 1990s and early 2000s. Developers built more than one billion square feet of space from 2000 to 2008 in the top markets, up by 25 percent compared to the same period in the 1990s.[47] That massive growth in retail space occurred in the same decade as the nation's slowest population growth in sixty years.[48] Decision makers recruited and promoted more retail space, even if there was already more retail square footage than could be supported. This retail push persisted when commercial real estate started to move from malls to mixed-use projects with ground-floor retail (generally mixed with housing, offices, or other activities on floors above).

In many communities, policies have changed since 2010 and now require ground-floor retail in most new city center or suburban town center buildings. To be clear, mixed-use projects with retail on the ground floor are still better than single-use retail malls at the edge, but they must be done thoughtfully. Mixed-use projects earn 12 percent higher rents on their commercial space on average and increase in value more than similar commercial-only properties in the surrounding market.[49] In addition, in strong market areas, mixed-use projects earn a retail lease premium of 15 to 25 percent more than the surrounding retail.[50] Even if the mix is needed, however, we also need to think about the details in an area: where do people really gather in town, how do we place different kinds of uses in different parts of our downtowns, what kinds of businesses make a long-term difference for our community's economy, and how can our main streets represent our demographics.

There is also a cost issue here. It is not just about oversupply of retail space overall (the really expensive peanut butter), but about the cost of using these new mixed-use spaces. The reality is that new construction—especially mixed-use projects with ground-floor retail—is really expensive. This means that the unintended consequence of requiring ground-floor retail in new multifloor projects is that the only business that can usually afford that ground-floor space is a national chain. As a result, everywhere looks the same, and the local small businesses are left behind. To counteract these trends, new development needs to carefully consider the changing market, how to stand out, and what it means to truly be a part of a community.

3 *Approval processes and requirements for new development are inconsistent.* Real estate development approval processes are different in every community. In many places, a developer can build "by right" what is in the zoning regulations, which means that a project would not require community review. In other places, building plans must be submitted for design review or go through a series of council and committee reviews before being approved. Developers can offer neighborhood improvements, like public space, as a proffer to the community in exchange for more density, or they may ask for a variance (an exception) to build something different than the zoning requires. In many places, the approval process is long, unpredictable, expensive, and highly political.

In hot markets, people with high incomes battle against new development and slow down approval processes. This NIMBY— not in my backyard—confrontation makes new real estate space even more expensive and out of the price range of local businesses.[51] High construction costs contribute to this issue, but unpredictable approval time lines and pressures to reduce density (the number of units in the project) also add to the square-foot cost of a project.

Rarely do community leaders think about how each piece of development serves the entire community. NIMBYism usually means that development gets pushed to areas without a strong advocacy base, particularly Black or Latino neighborhoods. Fights against adding apartment buildings or more housing to a neighborhood often have at their core racial and income discrimination.

Development decisions need community input, and they need to have input from all the impacted communities, not just the one with the loudest voice or the biggest team of lawyers, yet jurisdictions are set up to create significant unpredictability for developers in exactly this way. This process both increases the cost of the project (if there are delays) and provides inconsistent (at best) opportunities for underrepresented neighborhoods to have a voice in the process.

In contrast, in cooler markets, places that are not seeing investment interest, communities are often willing to take whatever a developer proposes without a fight for high-quality design. The community may have no design guidelines or requirements about the exterior of the building to make it fit into the downtown and feel look like it is a part of the place. As a result, the community gets a project that may look like one anywhere else in the country and that does not connect with the community. It might even have retail that sits empty because it's too expensive for the location and local businesses. This lack of confidence in the market, and lack of belief in the potential of the community, becomes a self-reinforcing outcome. Development is low quality, so it attracts low-quality investment. The place, and its decision makers, do not see the hometown as worthy, so the development does not help create a stronger, more loved place.

New development and rehabilitation of older buildings can be a lifeline for a community. If done with purposeful thought as to what a project should achieve, who will use it, and how the community will be engaged in the project from the start, everyone benefits.

These same challenges are reflected in the way many local governments run business development or assistance programs. All too often, we see an economic development program fail because, supposedly, "no one showed up" for the assistance, with the conclusion that the program wasn't needed (versus a conclusion that maybe the design of the program didn't take the detailed needs of the users into account). Sometimes we find that business development programs end up serving a predominantly White audience of business owners. Then we need to ask, is the program not reaching Black or Latino business owners because of a problem with outreach, public relations, or language? Or maybe it is because of the content of the program, its location, or a lack of trust between communities? We will never know what's wrong unless we talk directly with the people who are affected by the changes and bring in the support network of partners around them.

What Is at Stake?

Taken together, these economic development mistakes can indicate whether a place will thrive or not. The old-fashioned economic development approach, the problems and inequities that it created, and the stark economic reality we face due to COVID-19 mean that we are digging ourselves farther and farther into a hole.

Today, it's time to stop leaving people and places behind. It's time for a new model, one that invests in the true value of a place and its people; one that invests in all kinds of living wage jobs, supports local businesses, and works purposefully to close the racial wealth gap; one that creates a place where kids choose to stay or come back to as adults; one that builds our pride—pride of people and pride of place—that is so essential to a better path forward. We need a better local economic model.

That's the model we can create. Let's forge a better path forward.

An Inclusive New Economic Development Path to Invest
in People and the Places We Love

CHAPTER 3

A Stronger Economic Development Model with Small-Scale Manufacturing

The street was filled with people. Maybe you've seen something like this in your community: music playing, small canopies of bright colors covering vendors' tables, people wandering up and down the street in awe of all the interesting things made by people in their city. Food, drink, jewelry, beautiful cutting boards—it was all there. The amazing smells of foods from around the world filled the air.

I was wandering RemFest, the outdoor festival of the Remington neighborhood in Baltimore, Maryland. (Yes, it was before COVID-19, but we'll get back to festivals like this one day.) It was an event to celebrate the neighborhood and its residents. It drew people from all over the city, and the crowd reflected the diversity of Baltimore. Local vendors lined the street, and customers stood in line to support these businesses. People came with their families and danced to the live music. The smiles on people's faces made it clear that the event brought joy and gave people the chance to experience and celebrate their community.

In the 1970s, investment and government policy were driving people to the suburbs, to new tract development, and to private, separated properties. In the 1980s, we hollowed out our cities and took investments away from people who stayed—or couldn't leave.

All that changed in 2020. Before the COVID-19 pandemic, places across the United States were seeing new energy flow back into their downtowns and to their neighborhood main streets. Even in the time of COVID-19, cities are blocking off streets to cars so that children can play outside safely and restaurants can expand outdoors. People are craving ways to be together and to gather as part of their community. It is an essential part of who we are.

A number of small and medium-sized communities, such as Greenville, South Carolina, are growing in population and attracting businesses because they started to invest in their people and their place differently a while ago. Thrillist even started writing about the best small towns with awesome downtowns to move to.[1] This new reality requires a combination of placemaking investments, place-based economic development, and inclusive ecosystem building. In nontechnical terms, it means investing in places, people, and how they connect. That is how we change our economic development model to create strong, inclusive, local economies for the long-haul.

Building a New Model

Three fundamental tenets of this new economic development model are core to this work:

1 Investing in the place is key to economic strength.

2 A unique identity of the place is essential to long-term value.

3 Social connections are essential to economic resilience and the place's "stickiness."

And small-scale manufacturing businesses help us achieve that model.

Investing in Place Is Key to Economic Strength

Small-scale manufacturing businesses are wonderful in storefronts. They draw people to an area to see cool stuff made, they help attract investment to neighboring properties (especially when they are filling a vacant space), and they are uniquely of that place. No one else has that business owner, with that brand and that product, anywhere else. These businesses make people proud of their community, their main street, and their downtown. They often buy supplies locally, hire locally, and have deep roots in the community.

Every place (a neighborhood or downtown or main street) is stronger when it is loved by the people who live there. You know that a place is loved when you see it. Storefronts are cared for, and people gather and spend time there. It isn't about property value. Rather, it's about pride in the place in small and important ways.

For instance, does the neighborhood have its own festivals and gatherings? Do people say that they come from that neighborhood or that city with pride? Do residents feel that the place is invested in by the district authority, local government, or local businesses?

There are a million ways—many of which are very low budget—to invest in a place, but it takes the community coming together to make it happen. Do we want gardens in vacant lots? Stoops or sidewalks swept clean by business owners? Public places where people can gather? What does it look like to walk down the street? Are storefronts filled with activity and open for consistent hours?

These acts signal to the property owners and to local business owners that this place is worthy of investment. Each act is a small way to invest in that place. These acts signal to local residents that it is a place to spend time and money.

Local leadership investing in the place is essential to economic success. And that includes public, private, and political investment in that place.

For instance, many communities work to implement the elements of complete streets—wider sidewalks, traffic calming, and landscaping—and places for the community to gather in plazas downtown. These investments signal to property and business owners that a place is worthy of their time and money. For example, Lancaster, California, saw an increase in investment in downtown worth ten times the investment that the city put into these kinds of elements. For the $10.6 million the city invested in wider sidewalks, landscaping, a plaza for people to stroll, and steps to slow traffic, the private sector invested $126 million in the area. The city had a 26 percent increase in sales tax revenue from this area, and the community added eight hundred jobs.[2]

We also need to acknowledge that some places might be loved by their residents but neglected by the local jurisdiction. The local budget might be shrinking, and it costs money to take care of a downtown or a neighborhood main street. The properties on main street might be owned by distant investors who neglect maintenance. Some main streets may not be maintained because the jurisdiction doesn't see them as an essential investment. We know that there is a historic, as well as present-day, difference in how much a city invests in different neighborhoods because of race. It is visible in many communities.

Are there certain neighborhoods where the garbage piles up in front of businesses? Are there vacant lots? Is there litter? Are there festivals, but only ones directed at bringing in people from outside the community or for tourists? In a smaller city or town, does community investment go only to new commercial development at the edge of the jurisdiction? In a town with one main street, do the storefronts only include White-owned businesses and not businesses from the racial and ethnic diversity of its population? These issues all illustrate different kinds of neglect, different ways of saying that certain people and certain places are more important than others.

In 2017, the City of Baltimore Planning Department looked back at its past five years of capital investment in neighborhoods—the money the city spends to build schools, fix roads, renovate libraries, and widen sidewalks (all the stuff we see). The research showed that the capital projects in neighborhoods that are predominantly (at least 75 percent) White were funded on average at $15 million, whereas the average project investment in predominantly Black neighborhoods was $8 million. The bias was even more extreme across income lines. In neighborhoods with poverty rates greater than 40 percent, the average project investment was $3.5 million, whereas neighborhoods with poverty levels less than 20 percent received investments averaging $14 million.[3] Residents of Baltimore's Black and lower-income neighborhoods were being left behind.

We need to focus efforts on how to invest in place in a way that are inclusive, meet the diverse needs of the neighborhood, and benefit the people in the neighborhood today. Small-scale manufacturing businesses from the neighborhood and surrounding areas can help fill those storefronts, help rebuild the belief in that place, and begin to attract investment or inspire other local businesses to locate nearby.

The Unique Identity of the Place Is Essential to Long-Term Value

Places that are unique make us feel like we are somewhere special. That difference, that special sauce, that thing that makes it stand out—whatever it is that makes it the place it is—draws us in and makes us want to spend time there.

Think about a place you've been that feels different and special. It might be a small rural town or a neighborhood in a big city. The uniqueness of the place makes you curious about what you might see that you won't see somewhere else. That the place is special makes us feel special and gives us a boost of energy. It doesn't matter if it is our own hometown main street or one we choose to visit.

Some real estate developers pay big dollars to create an "authentic" experience, recognizing that it will draw future development and investments. They know that it will draw tenants for apartments and customers for shops. Large developers create a destination, events, and a brand for a place before even launching sales of property or development.

EDENS, a national real estate developer, did exactly that when it launched Union Market in Washington, DC, in 2013 to create value in its property. The market is located in an old wholesale and distribution complex within a five-minute walk of a subway station. The area is historic—the market was established by President Abraham Lincoln—and in recent years the market has housed international wholesale and import businesses, but with significant vacancies.

EDENS invested its own money to create an identity for the property that would make it a desirable destination. It chose to launch Union Market, the first modern food hall in the city. The development company filled the hall with local food companies showcasing the international flavors of the nation's capital, a produce stand, and an independent retailer that carries locally produced household goods. To bring people to this area that had previously been only wholesale operations and parking lots, EDENS created a wide variety of programming, both inside the market (from neighborhood meetings to "Mom Mornings") and in its neighboring parking lot (from music to artisan vendor festivals). Union Market drew people to an area where people did not just hang out before and gave them a reason to linger, shop, eat, and have new experiences.

By recruiting local food vendors and retailers from all over the city, EDENS created a DC-specific, unique identity for the area. New businesses that are not found anywhere else in the city opened at the market and in the surrounding blocks. EDENS spent five years creating this brand and promoting it intensively before breaking ground on residential development. It increased the property value for all surrounding future development by creating and promoting this unique destination.

These kinds of places also occur naturally and in many cases are threatened by redevelopment because of their success. Little Haiti in Miami, Florida, is an example. In the 1970s and 1980s, Haitians fled their country to escape poverty and oppression, and many settled in this affordable

Miami neighborhood. They put down roots and started restaurants and businesses. They created art and held celebrations of their Haitian heritage.[4] Today, the murals and art on the streets make it clear that you are visiting a place with a special heritage. The area was so successful that it won an official designation from the city to be named Little Haiti. The neighborhood has its own cultural center, food marketplace, musical performances, Haitian creole restaurants, and bookstores.[5] It is a place that stands out and feels special.

Such areas are also a strong draw for investment. When some of the naturally occurring places are so successful, business owners are threatened with being priced out of their own neighborhoods if the local businesses don't own their properties. To counteract this trend, we need to plan for wild success that doesn't leave people behind and retains that special sauce.

Your history, your people, and your local business owners are what makes your downtown or main street special. It might be naturally occurring in your community, but you didn't really notice it as an asset before. Each place needs purposeful work to create this in a way that is inclusive so that we are building up the local economy, not displacing it. And small businesses (especially small-scale manufacturing businesses) can be a way to ensure that everyone in your community feels that this opportunity to build the local economy and build community wealth is available to them.

Highlighting the identity of your community and being inclusive require asking some questions. Who are the people in your storefronts? Who do they represent? Who owns the businesses? How are they designed on the front and inside to reflect the personality of the owner and of the community? How is this business specific to your place and region? How is it specific to the neighborhood and the people who live there? Most important, when you look around, do you know if you are in a specific place?

Answering these questions should reveal a place that will reflect the community and retain value over time. This main street with unique businesses cannot be replaced with a new mall with national chains down the road because is no other place like it in the world.

Social Connections Are Essential
to Economic Resilience and Stickiness

The connections between business owners and people in the community are essential to economic resilience. Many types of connections matter, but personal, social connections draw people to a place and make them want to stay (its stickiness). These connections can also be important when a community needs to adapt and recover in the face of disaster.

Researchers have found that personal connections between business owners are important to the business's survival in the face of national disasters. Local business owners with strong connections to other owners were more likely to survive crises and reopen after a disaster, whereas those with fewer connections were more likely to go out of business.[6] The people with connections bartered services or deferred payments because of their social capital with the other business owners. Their social connections made them 24 percent more likely to be resilient than owners with weak connections.[7] Those connections become even more important when the economy is unpredictable or weak, as seen during the COVID-19 pandemic.

These connections can be important to a business's success even in stable times because these business owners can learn from and lean on one another, as often seen with startup programs working with cohorts of business owners. Successful programs also provide strong connections to expert mentors. A study of New York City tech startups found that businesses with strong personal connections to successful founders and with strong mentors were more than twice as likely to succeed as those without strong connections.[8] Places that invest purposefully in these cohorts and connections reap the benefit of stronger small businesses and, with direct action, could result in a more inclusive and diverse community of business owners. Cohorts for Black-owned businesses, for example, can offer support and help owners overcome barriers to launch and create strong local businesses.

Attachment to a place (its stickiness) is also essential to its economic survival. Why do people stay in the town or city if they could have the opportunity to go somewhere else? In a study called "Soul of the Community," the Knight Foundation and Gallup found that there are three major reasons people stay in a community:[9]

1 People feel included.

2 There are places to gather.

3 The place has a beauty in its buildings or natural environment.

This connection is not about economic opportunity. It's not about salaries. It's about connections—emotional and physical—and inclusion.

In the end, however, the result for the city is about money. That same study found that places with a higher stickiness factor also had higher rates of growth in gross domestic product (GDP), with the rate of growth exceeding the population rate of growth by two and a half to three times.[10]

We see this distinction echoed in real estate studies: people are attracted to locations that have places to walk to and gather and to places that have that special something. The National Association of Realtors surveys people every two years about community preferences to help its members understand trends in what attracts households. This survey is a window into changing preferences. In the 2017 survey, the most recent, some of the top priorities for people deciding where to live included homes that are an easy walk to places like shops and parks and communities that have safe sidewalks.[11] These preferences were echoed in an Urban Land Institute housing study of millennials, which showed that community character and proximity to shopping rank among the top priorities when these younger adults decide where to live.[12]

We need all three of those fundamental parts listed above—inclusion, gathering spaces, and beauty—to build a strong local economy. We also need to invest in the place; we need to show who we are and the inclusive, unique sauce of our community; and we need to help business owners continue to build stronger connections. That's the way to create a place that people want to stay and invest in, as well as a place that will attract other investments and entrepreneurs.

We will only achieve these outcomes with purposeful actions that will benefit residents from the entire community, attract businesses and people, and strengthen the local economy. That feeling of being included, of feeling valued, of feeling connected to others in our community, does not happen automatically. And for our business owners, it doesn't happen across racial and ethnic lines without concrete, intentional actions from city leadership.

Steps to a New Path Forward

So how do we move forward? We're here (or at least I am) because there are a lot of people still dragging places down with the old default model and leaving people and places behind. They are wondering why their local economies are losing momentum or even stalling out (even before COVID-19 hit). And now people and places are struggling. It is time for us to forge a new path forward that goes well beyond filling in a missing piece of the local economy.

Here are four major actions to build a stronger, more resilient local economy:

1 Invest in people who live in our community now.

2 Invest in target locations, like downtown, main streets, and neighborhood centers.

3 Create a structure to support, scale up, and invest in those people and those places.

4 Think long term, but act now.

Let's first go over these different ways to create a strong economy for more people. Then we'll talk about how small-scale manufacturing helps us get there.

Invest in People Who Live in Your Community Now

When economic development strategies are based solely on recruiting outside businesses and "talent," the community gets the message that it doesn't have what or who it needs to make a thriving place. It means the local leaders do not believe in the potential and skills of the people already there.

Are local economic leaders focusing on recruitment because they are hunting for one big company to come save the economy, or does the community have a competitive advantage in one sector that they are building on? The intention and purpose make a difference.

What if the local leaders do believe in the residents? What if they provide access to resources to help community residents become thriving business owners and employees and show that they are dedicated to the community for the long term? A local government might prioritize funding for a small-business incubator or a local investment fund for growing businesses instead of building a new access road to a big-box store with minimum-wage jobs.

If the local government invests in the people and places in its community, those investments will not leave town (as many larger employers do over time). Residents, especially small-scale manufacturing business owners, often have deep roots in the community and are unlikely to pick up and move a business.

The benefit of local investment can be seen in a number of different ways. In one study of small businesses in Maine, researchers found that local businesses spent 45 percent of their revenue in the surrounding counties and another 9 percent in other parts of the state, with more than 50 percent of all spending benefiting the state and local community; the typical big-box store spends about 14 percent in the state and local economy, pulling the rest out of the region.[13] A report from the Better Business Bureau found that 68 percent of the spending of locally owned businesses stays in the community.[14] That spending is direct reinvestment in the community from the businesses and the owners who live there.

This kind of investment also draws customers. Some cities survey their downtown visitors to better understand what attracts them to the area and the importance of these local businesses. A survey of the Andersonville neighborhood in Chicago, Illinois, found that 95 percent of customers said that locally owned businesses were an important factor in deciding to shop or go to a restaurant in the area.[15]

Local businesses are the identity of a neighborhood. Investing in the people and the businesses who live there just makes economic sense.

Invest in Target Locations:
Downtown, Main Streets, and Neighborhood Centers

Placemaking means to make a place that is distinct and to invest in a place where people can come together. The subject gets a lot of coverage in the media and in real estate, economic, and planning trade materials, and many communities are working on placemaking in their downtowns. They know that a strong downtown is essential to a strong local economy.

Targeting one location does not mean that others will be neglected; rather, it means that we work on implementing changes and taking action in that one place with a burst of energy to be a catalyst and show people what is possible. When we focus on a target location, residents can quickly see the impact and get excited about getting involved in what comes next. It also allows us to try a new idea in one place to see if it works before we roll it out to the rest of the jurisdiction. When we target locations for investment, we can be more effective, lower the risk of investments, and create success faster for our local small businesses than when we spread our energy out over multiple locations.

In a small town, making these investments on main street may be enough. In larger cities, though, it may be necessary to also invest in neighborhood main streets. These local main streets were often the commercial center of the neighborhood. In many communities, these places were neglected as cities emptied out in the 1970s and 1980s, especially in predominately Black neighborhoods. Today, these same places are an amazing opportunity for locally owned businesses to move into storefronts and build wealth for a local household. We need to make it a priority to target neighborhood centers and work with the residents to bring these places back to life. We need to do it with purpose and intent to break from the old model and the systemic racism that neglected these places and do things differently. If we do not think purposefully about who benefits from investment, we leave people and places behind.

Unfortunately, it is still common to see investment directed at wealthier White communities, as mentioned earlier in the study of investment in Baltimore. Another study looking at St. Louis, Missouri, found that government tools such as Tax Increment Finance incentives were pulling investment away from predominantly Black neighborhoods in the city.[16] Another study found that cities that are more segregated spend less on public services throughout the entire city compared to cities that are less segregated that spend more on public services on average.[17]

Cities often continue to invest more in the neighborhood centers that are already thriving. These places bring in tax revenue, and the city wants that to continue. Yet these places are thriving because of historic investments in that place. A struggling neighborhood center has likely been neglected for generations. Areas that were redlined in the 1930s are generally still more economically distressed, with lower household incomes, lower housing values, and lower rents,[18] than areas that were not redlined. If local leaders want to invest in places that are already doing well—so that they do even better—the neglected neighborhood main streets are unlikely to ever catch up.

It is important to think about what purpose we are trying to achieve with these investments. And we need to do so with fresh eyes at historic injustices and the systemic racism baked into our economic development and planning decision-making.

Who should benefit from the investments in downtown? Who should benefit from neighborhood main street investments? What outcomes are we trying to achieve? How do we invest in a place with the neighborhood residents and lift up its main street in partnership?

Community organizations like BakerRipley worked with residents in the Gulfton-Sharpstown and East Aldine neighborhoods in Houston, Texas, to understand what the residents of each neighborhood needed to be able to build household wealth, live healthy lives, and have better access to resources. Starting in 2005 in Gulfton-Sharpstown, a dense and diverse neighborhood with residents from more than eighty countries and a significant Latino population, and replicating the process in 2018 with East Aldine, a neighborhood of second-generation Mexican Americans, the organization conducted hundreds of interviews with residents and business owners to understand their specific needs. The result was two completely different kinds of community centers for two different neighborhoods: one in Gulfton-Sharpstown that provides a health center, charter school, and credit union; and one in East Aldine that is home to a makerspace and an incubator for neighborhood-owned businesses.[19]

When thinking about where investment will be directed, we need to ask some specific questions. Where has investment gone historically? Which communities have been overlooked? How do we invest in target locations in a way that expands opportunity for more people? These questions need to be answered honestly. If not, more people and places will be left behind. But with inclusive and targeted investments in these places—the physical structure and the small businesses in them—we can start to change the conversation.

Create a Structure to Support, Scale, and Invest in People and Places

No one succeeds on their own. And no place succeeds wildly without intervention. Anyone who tells you otherwise is selling something.

Each entrepreneur, each business, each thriving place has benefited from countless inputs, investments, and support from different parts of the world around them. The ecosystem may be one built by generations of investment or one that the business owner hunted down and built piece by piece, but somewhere and somehow the support structure around a business made a difference in its success. As mentioned earlier in the chapter, research shows that businesses that support one another are more successful and more resilient than those that do not have such connections.

This structure or ecosystem is something we can purposefully build—for local entrepreneurs, their businesses, and the places we want them to thrive. We can think about it as a continuum of support—something that's been promoted nationally for tech entrepreneurs, but rarely provided to local small-scale manufacturing businesses or even places.

In the tech world, there are startup incubators (nonprofit, providing wraparound help and space), accelerators (business that helps and invests in the potentially high growth business), mentors, pitch competitions to investors, and programs to help these businesses grow and scale up. We need to provide this same structure to more people who need it. That means acting with purpose.

Let's get really specific here. If we want to make a difference in our communities and help more people thrive, we need to provide this same kind of business support to other kinds of businesses, not just tech. The continuum of support works, but it will need to be adapted to the specific needs of the community, the people who live there, and business type.

We need to ask specific questions upfront. Who should benefit from the small-business programming? Whose businesses should thrive? What are their specific needs? If your answer is "local business owners," you are not getting specific enough.

Different small-business owners, from different backgrounds, incomes, experiences, and education, will need different kinds of support. The standard start-up training might not serve business owners who do not have college degrees. The regional economic development authority might host startup training boot camps, but they may not be accessible by transit and thereby excluding a major part of the local population. The startup program might be held in English even though major parts of the entrepreneurial community are recent immigrants and need training programs in Spanish or another language. Or the local area may have an accessible startup program, but the only business support program to help small and successful businesses scale up faster and grow might have a minimum revenue requirement that a local entrepreneur might not meet yet.

Would a downtown in one community that is thriving from years of investment and a neighborhood main street in another community that has been neglected for decades need the same kind of ecosystem support to be strong contributors to our local economy? That's unlikely. The same goes for our businesses.

When we talk about who we want to benefit from the investment—in this case, the investment is in the structure and programming—we can understand in detail what we need to build to support these people and places. For example, in Marion, North Carolina, the local government wanted to bring investment back to downtown and increase the number of locally owned small businesses there, so the city, its downtown business association, the local chamber of commerce, and the local small-business center launched the Growing Entrepreneurs Marion program in 2016 to do just that. The program has two major parts. The first is an eight-week program to teach people how to launch a business and develop an actionable business plan specific to opening in downtown Marion. Then, businesses that complete the program can go on to the second part and apply for a $5,000 grant to pay for rent and utilities to open their business in a downtown storefront. Through this targeted investment, property and business owners invested more than $2 million and added forty-five jobs to downtown over three years—all in a town with fewer than eight thousand residents.[20] That's a targeted impact. This kind of focused structure helps the business owners, the property owners, and the city achieve their shared goals: a vibrant downtown with successful businesses from the community.

Think Long Term, but Act Now

Some of the ideas that come out of this work are going to be challenging and hard to do. They may be very different from anything the community has ever done before. They may mean that local leaders do things really differently for a long time. And that's great, because we need aspirations to move us in big ways. Complacency will never result in a thriving place.

At the same time, however, we can't wait for the big ideas and the long-term plans to happen and expect them to fix everything. We need to find the hundreds of little steps we can take now to move in that direction. We need to find partners who can help with all those steps. And we need to excite people along the way about these steps. State them publicly. Take pictures. Give accolades. Tell the media.

All the little steps, these short-term wins, are proof of things changing. They show the community that this work will not result in just another round of planning fatigue or empty promises to the neighborhood. These wins are public, celebrated, and shared.

Many businesses use these same principles to build momentum for success. The short-term wins help employees get excited about the work and show them how to realize the potential of the project. The wins help them see that their work adds up to something tangible.

Short-term wins—clear, unambiguous wins (not window dressing or hand waving, but real wins)—show people that the work is valid and building momentum. The wins keep people engaged and decrease the power of any nay-sayers. In the words of professor and entrepreneur John Kotter, these wins are "proof of progress."[21]

The wins will build support for our big crazy outcomes. We need people to see the benefits and live the benefits every step of the way. Then we can achieve our big crazy goal over the long term.

Through discussions with business owners during one project with The Loop, a community improvement district along a corridor in Columbia, Missouri, we identified the need for a commercial, shared kitchen. Within two months of the project's finish, The Loop announced a partnership with the Regional Economic Development Inc. (the regional authority) to create a space and identified a location on the corridor. A month later, The Loop secured the lease for the space and announced a partnership of twelve organizations to create a mission-driven commercial shared kitchen. The Loop partners promoted these wins on their websites, but more importantly, they worked with the local media to announce these wins in the local newspaper. By promoting those immediate wins publicly and with enthusiasm, they built excitement and energy for the new space and found more people who wanted to be involved in it.

These actions change how we build our local economy. They help us make a place that people love and that has a strong and resilient economy, in a way that builds wealth for more people.

The Exciting Potential of Small-Scale Manufacturing

Small-scale manufacturing businesses can help you make these four pieces of the new economic model become a reality. These businesses can help each community create a thriving and unique place. They can help build an inclusive economy in which more people have the opportunity to build wealth. They can be brought into the work quickly to help achieve short-term and visible wins. This business type is not a solution for all our community challenges, but it can make a big difference in solving more of them, and faster.

The reality is that most communities are not using all the local assets available to them to be successful. In fact, most communities are doing this work with at least one hand tied behind their back. And in many cases, one of the local assets not engaged, a major missing piece, is small-scale manufacturing businesses. (Remember that small-scale manufacturing businesses are ones that create a tangible product that can be replicated or packaged, across any material, be it hot sauce, handbags, or hardware.)

Although the Small Business Administration defines "small business" as one with fewer than five hundred employees, small-scale manufacturing is much smaller. In most communities, this business sector is in the "microenterprise" category, with one to twenty employees, so that it can fit into the existing buildings in and around downtown. In larger cities, where existing building spaces may be larger, small-scale manufacturing may be as large as fifty employees. Most important is that these businesses fit into spaces in our downtowns, main streets, and neighborhoods because they are modern production businesses—clean, quiet, and great neighbors.

Small-scale manufacturing businesses are an untapped asset for downtown and main street. We can achieve many more of our purposeful outcomes faster when we include this missing business sector in our work.

Picture it:

1 Main Street is full of people and businesses. The storefronts are no longer vacant. Small-scale manufacturing businesses filled the first shops when there was no foot traffic and attracted people to come visit and see things being made.

2 Local businesses bring outside revenue into the community. Local product businesses sell online and wholesale (throughout

the region and nationally) and bring sales dollars back into the community—buying supplies locally, hiring locally, and paying taxes locally.

3 Locally owned businesses are paying a living wage to more residents. The product businesses pay 50 to 100 percent higher wages than service or retail jobs. We help more people out of poverty and start closing the racial wealth gap.

4 People from nearby neighborhoods who made products at home are now in storefronts. They are a part of the success, not displaced by it. Our residents thrive because of our investments. They are valued. They build family wealth.

5 Our community of business owners represents the demographic diversity of our community. Small-scale manufacturing businesses from every part of our community are supported in the way they each need so that they can be part of this thriving economy.

6 Support of local business owners attracts more entrepreneurs to the community. Word of mouth spreads that this place, this community, believes in people who create products. People hear about the thriving place with successful businesses and want to be a part of it. More entrepreneurs come to town.

7 Main streets and downtown are valued and worthy of investment. Property owners fix up old storefronts. Parks are cleared and cleaned. Programming brings people together. The place is loved by the residents and the local government.

I'm betting you can picture those things too.

And no, bringing small-scale manufacturing businesses into the work is not going to make all those outcomes happen tomorrow. It will take a lot more than that. But those businesses are essential to creating that future, one that is inclusive, strong, and proud.

How Does It All Come Together?

We know that it is necessary to invest in people and place and build a support structure to help businesses and the places thrive. So what does it look like when we bring small-scale manufacturing into the mix?

Remember that small-scale manufacturing businesses can fill storefronts and help more people become business owners or earn better wages than retail or service jobs. These businesses allow people to show their pride in who they are, what they can make, and where they come from. The business type is inclusive—there are producers in every part of our communities.

In many communities, however, there are a number of barriers to this future. For example, the zoning for downtown may not allow artisan manufacturing in the storefronts, downtown may be neglected by distant owners, business development programs may not serve small-scale manufacturing businesses, or space might be too expensive. But we can solve those problems.

By investing in small-scale manufacturing, business owners, and space for them in our downtowns, we have a new way to invest in the people and places in our communities. By pursuing a new model, we can acknowledge the value of the people in our community and in the places of our community and build a stronger, more resilient, more inclusive local economy.

Are we bold enough to make this a reality? Do we believe in our community and our people enough to make this happen? How will we focus on the new path forward and take different steps to make this aspiration become our reality?

Recast City's five-step method is where we start.

Small-Scale Manufacturing in Our Storefronts

CHAPTER 4

Five Steps to Recast Your City

Wᴇ ᴋɴᴏᴡ ᴛʜᴀᴛ ᴛʜᴇ ᴏʟᴅ ᴅᴇғᴀᴜʟᴛ method leaves people and places behind. We know that we want to do better and find a new path forward. So how do we do it?

Recast City's five-step method will help you turn that corner and create a new path to inclusive economic success for your city by focusing on small-scale manufacturing.

Local leaders who use this method are done with boom-and-bust economies. They are ready to say that there is no single big solution to fix it all, and they will put in the work to help more people in more places with a new economic development model.

This method means talking to new people (ahh!), listening in new ways (oooh!), and pulling in new ideas on which to act. It gets you and your team to focus on a few key pieces:

⚙ Understand how your downtown can reflect the awesome uniqueness of your community.

⚙ Bring different people to the table and meet at different tables.

⚙ Collect information in a new way based on user research.

⚙ Implement discrete, short-term actions that move toward big, long-term outcomes.

Through it all, small-scale manufacturing needs to be part of the work.

Here are the steps in brief. The details about how to conduct each step follow in subsequent chapters.

Step 1: Light the Spark

The first steps require you to understand what you have in your community and describe the outcomes you want to achieve through the economic development strategy, real estate investment, or programming for entrepreneurs.

Pretty basic, right? Well, only sort of.

In this step, you will work with a small group of instigators (the people setting this project in motion, such as local government leaders, the local community development corporation, the business improvement district) to understand the context, urgency, and major outcomes you want to achieve as you recast your city. You will begin to build a list of assets and partners to involve in this work. This is called the Spark. Think of it as the first brain dump (with structure) to make sure that the entire starting team for the project has a shared understanding of what is going on in the community, what you are trying to achieve, and what major outcomes are essential for success.

As we discussed in chapter 3, you may begin to ask, where should the investment go? Who lives there now? How should those people benefit from the investment? Who else needs to be at the table to make sure the benefit reaches the people and the place in need?

The Spark stage creates a shared foundation of knowledge in which the local project will grow. It is essential to the success of the investment. Remember that every time we spend public or philanthropic dollars on economic development and our downtowns, it is an investment. We are working to make something happen for the public good. No more trickle-down benefits (that is, if we spend it all on a big business, someday it will reach the little ones). As we discussed in the new model in chapter 3, it is important to pick where the work will be focused: downtown, main street, or a neighborhood center.

At this stage, start with a clear understanding of why we need to take on this work and who should benefit from it. We will learn a lot more about specific needs through the next steps, but let's start by being clear about who should benefit and which places need the focus. For instance, saying that we want the "entire city" to benefit from a new economic development strategy—such as a startup program—is like Apple, when releasing the first iPhone, saying that it wanted the "public" to buy it. Apple knew that there would be early adopters, so it focused its marketing on the characteristics of those early adopters.

If our local economic development program wants to benefit the "entire city," it will leave out most people. Most likely, the startup programming will be directed, by the old default model, to whichever community the local leaders know already. Startup programs predominantly benefit White middle- to upper-class individuals who are already plugged into the local government systems of support. Most often, it means that a generic startup program will not benefit the people most in need of entrepreneurial help, which includes groups of people who have been underrepresented in business development programming in the past, often our Black, Latino, and immigrant communities. And this cycle will keep happening unless we work to find a specific geographic area or population most in need of the investment.

This first step will help you focus on the community and the places that need to succeed and help to ensure that they actually benefit from the investment. Too many places waste money aimlessly on programs and have no idea why they don't work or why they don't help change the outcomes in their community. That practice stops when we recast our city.

Once we understand who or where is in need of investment, we can also talk about specific benefits. When you finish this project or program or strategy, what is that outcome? What does it look like? How do you experience it?

Working together, we can understand the opportunity and urgency for this work and begin to define specific outcomes in this step so that we know what we need to achieve. We will also begin to understand which partners will be essential to help us both reach the people in need and implement the changes at the end of the project. We'll get into the details of all these questions and how to navigate this step in chapter 5.

Step 2: Find and Connect with New People

Finding and connecting means getting out of your office and talking to new people. Each person has their own circle of connections, and by nature, that circle will always be limited. Few people can know every person in their community. So whenever we want to collect information about our community, we have the danger of only turning to the people we know for input.

We see this all the time: in "public meetings," where the same set of people show up to complain every time; or in local government small-business programming, where the same population shows up for support. It is common for the same small group of businesses to benefit from local funding because they are "in the loop." It just means that they know the systems—and other people don't.

Unfortunately, the loop often breaks down along racial and ethnic lines. Local government business programs historically benefited White-owned businesses, once on purpose and now primarily by default. Real estate development benefited those who could afford the price point of the new product, without regard to how the neighborhood residents would be included and feel ownership of the new space.

But here's the thing—a diversity of voices is essential to understand the needs of your community. If you want to save your downtown or main street, the people who live and work in and around that place need to be at that table.

In my work across the United States, I have found that even the most well-intentioned local leaders struggle to bring new people to the table. Often, they don't know people across racial, ethnic, and economic lines. They have not built enough of those trusting relationships yet.

This second step of finding and connecting with new people is essential because we need to find people with whom we do not have existing relationships. We need to find people who can give us new information about what works and doesn't work in our community.

Finding new people means finding business owners from small-scale manufacturing, home-based businesses in the target location, local property owners, and other local successful business owners who want to make a difference. It means finding out who is already working with startups or scaling businesses, who else is part of the business development ecosystem, and who might be a great asset for it.

We won't find all these people easily, however, which brings us to the Connectors. Connectors are trusted leaders from different communities who are willing to make change happen. They believe in that community and believe in its potential. These people might be faith leaders, cultural or civic leaders, or other trusted members of the community. They will be essential for your work. I promise. (We'll get into it more in chapter 6.)

Step 3: Start the Conversation with Interviews

The interview step gives us an opportunity to do a number of things:

- ⚙ Collect quantitative and qualitative information about our target beneficiaries (those we want to benefit from the investment).

- ⚙ Build a personal relationship with a new person in our target audience.

⚙ Build buy-in for implementation at the end of our process.

⚙ Go onsite in key locations to see firsthand how spaces and businesses operate.

The interview method is based on both political organizing and user research techniques. Why political organizing? The answer is because every decision in our community—about who benefits from local government investment and new real estate projects—is political. It is political in how decisions are made. And it is political in who benefits from that spending. So who gets interviewed, the diversity of those voices, and the importance of those voices all impact the needs we understand from the project, as well as how we implement the work.

We use interview techniques that originate in user research so that we get consistent and open information from people. But we need to organize the people to interview with an eye toward getting the voice of the target audience out in the open. We need to make sure that the needs of Black, Latino, and other business owners of color come through clearly, especially when those needs are different from other groups' needs.

We also bring the decision makers into the discussion early on so that they can fingerprint the process—that is, see their fingerprints on what we are creating and how we create it. At this time, we ask for their advice and input to shape how we will achieve the outcomes.

We'll get into detailed interview questions and techniques in chapter 7, but note that the interviews take place in the person's place of business or in the community space of their Connector (the trusted person who brought them into the conversation). Onsite interviews may not be possible during the COVID-19 shutdown, but it is an essential part of the work wherever possible.

To be clear, this step does not involve a series of big public meetings in the town hall. Rather, it is all about building personal relationships and trust, which means that we go to the businesses and the people wherever they are based to interview them and get their input.

Step 4: Analyze the Input

Step 4, analyze the input from the interviews and meetings, may seem obvious. Now is when we listen carefully, pull out assets that come up in conversation, and identify the gaps that still remain. Some people call this step a SWOT analysis—for strengths, weaknesses, opportunities, and threats—but we see it a little differently because we talk to new people with very specific outcomes in mind.

Our analysis focuses on those outcomes we set out to achieve at the start. Let's say that our outcome was to provide more space for Black and Latino producers on main street. Then, in the analysis, we found that the cost of renting the space is a barrier. Now is when we get into the details to see if it is because the businesses do not have the credit history and are therefore considered high risk for the lease or if distant landowners are sitting on empty storefronts.

One reason that we push into these kinds of questions is to craft actions (next steps) to address the gaps in current economic development and planning efforts and respond to specific needs. Please note: This step requires an open mind and a team willing to think through and understand both what was said in an interview and want is inferred or left unsaid. People may talk about being unaware of city programs available to small businesses. The question you will need to answer during your analysis stage is, why? Is it an outreach issue, a public relations challenge, or messenger and trust challenge? Each requires very different actions, so you should listen carefully and openly.

Chapter 8 includes a series of questions to help you uncover gaps and the assets that can make the biggest difference to achieve your outcomes. Also presented there are examples from communities that successfully made changes.

Step 5: Act Now

This final step, to act now, may seem obvious, but at the end of all this talking and thinking, we need to act. We need to identify short-term actions that will help us build for long-term change.

The actions should be limited in scope and be able to get kicked off in the next three to nine months. An action can be very small, but it needs to be SMART—specific, measurable, actionable, realistic, and timebound. For instance, if the people leading a project did not originally have strong relationships with community Connectors to a target population that should benefit from small-business development programming, they may determine after meeting with members of the target population (step 2) and getting their input (step 3) that building on those relationships should be a key first action.

The Knoxville Entrepreneur Center in Tennessee created immediate results along these lines by building a stronger relationship with the Knoxville Area Urban League. The two organizations now work together on small-business training programs and the annual citywide Maker Summit, which highlights producers of color in the community.

When Fremont, California, launched a project with the intention of building the pipeline of small-scale manufacturing businesses that could grow locally, the city found that it had no way to identify and bring these businesses into programming and space in the community. The city's first short-term win was to promote small-scale manufacturing businesses through all the city's public relations channels and ask business owners to sign up on a producers' list. This simple action attracted community attention and allowed the city to start bringing people together online and in meetups.

The actions can also build toward something bigger, such as a new commercial shared kitchen, coworking manufacturing space, a loan program for small producers, major zoning changes, or a procurement policy that targets local spending. These actions are discussed more in chapter 9.

This final, fifth step comes down to two precise actions. First, identify those short-term wins for the first three to nine months and then take action to build to the bigger stuff.

Why Does This Method Work?

Funding is scarce in local government and in local business, especially in the recovery and rebuilding of our local economies in times of emergency, like COVID-19. As a result, we need to talk to the target population to understand their greatest needs, not our perception of their greatest need. This part of the work helps us make sure that our investments are specific and in demand. It helps us make sure that the investment will help the people and the place, and it reduces our risk of failure.

In the past, many places spent lots of money on big actions that benefited only a few people. These actions rarely helped the population most in need. Sometimes the big projects were a complete waste of money. It is time to stop wasting money and make sure that our investments work.

All the actions to help our local businesses and invest in the selected places are built on actual needs from the community. The investments work because the Recast City method is built on a few basic values.

- We need to build trust in our communities. We do that by sitting down with people, one-on-one or in small groups. And we listen.

- We focus on really specific outcomes and specific benefits, not just on what but on who.

- We have those tough conversations.

- We stay laser-focused on short-term actions specific to those outcomes.

- We include small-scale manufacturing business owners—an economic engine sitting right under our noses—to expand opportunity quickly.

Columbia, Missouri, is a great example of the recast your city method at work. Columbia is a city of about 125,000 people halfway between Kansas City and St. Louis. It is home to the University of Missouri and according to 2019 US census figures is about 75 percent White-only and 25 percent Black, Latino, and other people of color.[1] About 95 percent of the population has a high school degree, and more than 50 percent have college or advanced degrees. Columbia has a fairly stable economy, with a downtown that belongs to the college students. The city has a lattice of highways that cross through town, dividing neighborhoods from downtown.

Our charge was to work with an area north of downtown, just south of the highway that cuts off the city center from the neighborhoods. This area, called The Business Loop (for the I-70 highway "loop" to its north), is a one-and-a-half-mile corridor lined with parking lots, car dealerships, bus parking, adult stores, and an electric utility. It is anchored at the west end by an old mall now being used as the base for the community college, and farther west at the highway interchange is a newer set of big-box stores. The area is lined with industrial and other forgotten spaces to the north (squeezed in between The Loop and the highway), and to the south is an older Black residential neighborhood of single-family homes.

Property owners along this corridor came together in 2015 and agreed to create a community improvement district (CID), which is like a business improvement district (BID), but just not downtown. The CID's stated outcome is to get local property owners, developers, and businesses to reinvest in The Loop and to include businesses that are underrepresented in downtown. Carrie Gartner, who had successfully reenergized the city's downtown by leading the BID, now leads the CID.

The CID worked with local property owners in 2017 and 2018 to come up with a plan for public spaces along the corridor that would start to make it a bit more pedestrian friendly. Currently, it is a thoroughfare for trucks cutting around the highway and has traffic on two lanes in each direction. But the group still didn't know what they wanted the area to be like, to feel like, as it grew. Zoning allowed for mixed-use development, but the busy road and the real estate market wouldn't support that cost of construction anytime soon.

We worked with the CID in 2019 to start the conversation about the business future of the corridor. Gartner recognized that the industrial area to the north was an asset and that she could build on that to create a place of business and community on The Loop.

The first step was to connect with property owners, small-product business owners, organizations supporting small businesses, and those working directly with entrepreneurs of color, especially Black and Latino business owners in the surrounding area. So, we interviewed more than sixty business owners and community leaders—from the Hispanic Chamber of Commerce, the Regional Economic Development Inc. Board (REDI), legacy businesses, immigrant communities, elected and appointed officials, the community college, and production businesses from micro to small (one to one hundred employees)—both in one-on-one and in small group interviews.

We briefed the community at a public meeting held in the neighborhood attended by 160 people. We found people who had always been at the table and also interviewed many people who had never been invited before to a conversation like that and didn't even know that there was a table. Gartner and The Loop's board of directors had their own one-on-one conversations with community Connectors to build trust and invite them to the interviews. We helped The Loop find those Connectors—community leaders and business leaders from the Black and Latino communities who hadn't been involved in economic development or business development efforts in the past—and it was the first time that the newly launched Hispanic Chamber of Commerce was involved in a city project. Our team met Black product business owners who had never benefited from local business development programming but who wanted to be involved in The Loop. Gartner and the board members asked these Connectors for introductions to more product business owners and expanded their relationships. In the process, we listened carefully to understand what was already working and what was missing.

The community vision came out clearly through the discussions. Each person articulated another part of the long-term vision for the area. People wanted a place where they could come together with their families, drop into a restaurant, and see local businesses that make them proud. People wanted to see the area be a job-creating center for the city with good wages that support families. They wanted investments to support the low-income neighborhood on one side of the corridor and the existing small industrial spaces on the other.

Business owners from a diversity of backgrounds shared their thoughts with us about having a business in Columbia. They told us about what worked and didn't work and about the resources and services they needed to grow their businesses. And people talked about their love of the city and the potential of this area. It was amazing.

The team then analyzed input from interviews, group discussions, the public event, meetings with the economic development board, and other local institutions. Based on the outcomes set at the start of the project, we settled on a set of short-term actions for The Loop:

⚙ Promote the work of artisan producers in the community, brand The Loop with this use, and bring them together for pop-up events to start drawing people to the area.

⚙ Fix the mixed-use zoning on the corridor to allow small-scale producers in existing structures and new development. The area was zoned for mixed-use development, with a fairly flexible set of uses, but small-scale production, even artisan production, was not one of the allowable uses.

⚙ Develop real estate examples of low-cost commercial development, including high-quality prefabricated buildings, to allow property owners to build space for producers at a lower cost than new mixed-use construction. (New construction would be too expensive for the lease rates that small producers could afford.)

⚙ Launch a mission-driven commercial shared kitchen for local microbusinesses because of the high demand for food-product business space and the need for immediate expansion. Focus the mission of the kitchen on serving local Black and Latino business owners.

Within one month of the project, The Loop CID launched a series of maker markets for the winter holidays, complete with activities for kids. Within two months, the CID met with the city administrator and got feedback on how to move forward with the zoning refinement. Within three months, it announced the commercial shared kitchen and started to negotiate a lease for the new space. And in 2020, The Loop opened the new shared kitchen.

Even in the face of the COVID-19 shutdown, The Loop promoted these businesses. They held Maker Monday auctions on Instagram, selecting three products from local producers to auction online each week. These products came from a diversity of business owners and helped keep these businesses in the public's eye even while stores were closed. Although the opening of the commercial shared kitchen was delayed, they are now open with a focus on supporting business owners of color in the region.

So yes, it is possible to identify desired outcomes, find and connect with the right people, understand their needs, and then act—all within months—with Recast City's five-step method. Are you ready? It's time to get started!

Find Your Hidden Assets: Makerspaces and Other Shared Work Spaces

CHAPTER 5

Step 1

Light the Spark

To create something better that works for more people, we need to start from a place of purpose. When we say that our goal is to "bring downtown back to life" or "redevelop Main Street," we are actually saying a million different things. In fact, often the conversation gets stuck at wonky terms like *walkable, livable,* or *community-oriented.*

But that doesn't get us very far. Each of those terms is vague. They conjure a different image in each person's mind, an image influenced by that person's background and experiences.

These phrases also leave many questions unanswered. Bring downtown back, but for whom? Who gets to define what is "livable" and for whom is it livable? Community-oriented toward which part of the community? Whose businesses get to be in the storefronts? Are we just leaving it to the "market" (which has been impacted by decades of policy and spending), or are we going to be purposeful about the place we create? The answers to all these questions affect the place we are creating and who will benefit from it.

The price point of each storefront lease, the type and size of shops, and even the design of the interiors and public space all impact the outcomes for our downtown. Our history of investment (or lack thereof) affects which places came back to life and which ones continue to struggle. Local versus distant property ownership in downtown also affects these outcomes.

When we start talking about downtowns and main streets, the questions of who will benefit and how we have a more inclusive process and create a more inclusive outcome rarely, if ever, are asked. So in many communities we end up in a default economic development scenario. We end up with network bias.[1]

What does network bias mean? It means that we turn to the people we already know. In this case, the people in charge of redeveloping downtown are likely to turn to the people who already benefit from the place. They turn to these existing relationships, or to other people with whom they already have some connection, to fill the storefronts and participate in the programming. Network bias also means that our brains take shortcuts based on past experiences—often subconsciously—and make assumptions about what people need.

It also means that the people and parts of our communities who are not well connected to those people—often underserved Black and Latino communities—will not benefit from the investments those decision makers control. It also means that business types, such as small-scale manufacturing businesses that often work under the radar and have not been part of the discussion before, are not invited into the discussion and continue operating isolated from the business community. So saying "redevelop downtown" just isn't enough.

We need to understand the context of the project—the urgency of doing this work—and define our outcomes and other pieces of our work in detail. To truly understand what is going on in our community, we need to push outside of our network bias and talk to new people.

In this first step of Recast City's five-step method, you set the stage and understand the baseline of what you have to work with. Like when Wesley says in *The Princess Bride*, "Well, why didn't you list that among our assets in the first place?" we need to know what assets we're working with at the start. We will add to those assets, and our understanding of them, throughout the process, but we need to start with a shared understanding of what we have.

This is the Spark step. It sparks everyone's thinking about key pieces essential for implementation. In fact, these same elements return in step 5, when we take action (chapter 8) to make changes happen quickly.

As you pick a target location in your community for this work—downtown, main street, a neighborhood center—think about why it's important to forge a new path forward. What kind of investments can you make in that place and in people in your community? Are you making a commitment to be purposefully inclusive in your outcomes to address past inequities in local economic development?

It is also the time to commit to economic development and investment decisions that will benefit every part of your local population—across race, ethnicity, and gender. For example, is your Main Street mostly filled with White-owned businesses while your population is very diverse? Then maybe your commitment is to make sure those storefronts represent the diversity of your community.

Do you have a lot of vacant storefronts in downtown, but you've never spoken to product businesses before? Then maybe your commitment is to diversify the businesses to include ones that are dynamic in-person but sell online (like product businesses) to bring new revenues into the community.

Does your city or county economic development authority only focus on recruitment and offer little to no support to help existing businesses scale up? Then maybe you will make a commitment to those existing businesses.

When we get this specific, do we risk failure? Absolutely. Whenever we put a statement out there—say, our outcome is to fill ten storefronts with business owners of color who succeed in this location for at least three years—we face a huge risk of failure. But it also means we have a real chance to succeed. We will never achieve that outcome unless we define it.

So what is your commitment to your community? You are reading this book because you want to make changes. You know that your community can be stronger, more inclusive, and show off what makes it special.

Let's be honest here. These outcomes might feel really big, which is understandable. But remember that the people and other community assets you discover through this method might introduce you to a whole new amazing part of your community. After all, you will talk to many, many people during the steps of this work. It is a gift to get to learn from more people in the community about their dreams for the place. You get the chance to ask people how they think you can get there as a community. You get the chance to build something together. But it takes leadership.

Politics are also involved. With any project, there is turf that could be crossed. Because of the nature of this work, leaders need to say that this specific place and these people need to be invested in and supported right now, not to the exclusion of others, but as the priority in relation to others. If your focus is on parts of that population that have not received much economic development and place-based investment in the past—often Black business owners and other business owners of color—targeted investments focused on those community members will be the priority.

If you are an elected official or municipal appointee, an outcome this specific says that you are making purposeful investments to achieve specific community outcomes. If you are a real estate developer, you're challenging yourself to think about how the neighborhood experiences this place so it starts and stays unique. If you're a downtown authority or business improvement district director, you have to say that you want something valued and specific, not just whatever any business wants.

Maybe you decide that the outcome is to invest in a space for microproducers who could grow into storefronts downtown. From interviews, however, you may find that the greatest need of microproducers is for a commercial shared kitchen. Only by setting an intention and then listening throughout the interviews will you understand these specific needs.

For example, will this commercial shared kitchen look and operate exactly like other shared kitchens? It probably won't; your community may need a canning line or a larger space to smoke meats. It will all be specific to your community based on information you gather in step 3, the interview. But when you light the Spark, you begin to think about the people already in your community and the kinds of outcomes you want to achieve.

These are tough conversations to have. But they are essential to the success of your work.

We need to make the conversations and questions more visible. We need to be clear and inclusive about our assets and our opportunities. We need to make fewer assumptions and fewer guesses, reduce our risk of failure, and get really specific about the opportunities to do something different.

The reality is that we make assumptions all the time without saying it out loud. When we launch a new startup program for the "public" or "to build entrepreneurship in our community," we make assumptions about the experience, education, and even access to internet that the program's customers will have. In fact, many of our local entrepreneurship programs assume a college education, experience in the business world, and strong internet access, which immediately leaves the vast majority of a community behind.

So instead of backing away from the hard conversations and just letting things happen, it is time to step up and be leaders. Be clear about what your community needs to thrive.

Thriving places include everyone—they don't leave people behind. Thriving places have creative people doing amazing things. Thriving places draw the attention of people from far and wide.

How are you going to do that? What are the pieces and who are the people already in your community that can help you wildly succeed?

Start Here

We start with a series of questions that you can use in conversations with the instigators of the project. These conversations can be with people in a neighborhood taking the lead to bring their main street back to life, economic development leaders from the jurisdiction, or the executive team of an improvement district—you get the idea. You want a small group of people who will shepherd this project from start to finish and are willing to do what it takes to make it happen.

One note about this small leadership group: please, please agree to be honest with one another about what needs to be done to get beyond the usual suspects (remember that network bias!). Be clear with one another about how to make real change in the immediate term in a way that has lasting impact. Don't just let old ideas slide into this new approach.

There are eight elements to set the Spark. These elements help you understand different parts about who needs to be at this new table, where you are heading (at least in general), and what assets you have to build on. As you work through these eight elements, you may also begin to identify gaps; keep them, too. In future steps, you will work to understand these gaps and which ones are most important to fix sooner rather than later to reach your outcomes.

Here are some of the questions to get started. For a complete worksheet with all the questions, download your copy at www.RecastYourCity.com.

Context: Describe what it is like to walk down the street in your project area. What is it like on a Saturday afternoon? What businesses do you see?

Urgency: Why is it important to make changes? What is at stake? What happens if you don't make any changes?

Outcomes: What should this place look like in five or ten years as you walk down the street? Who should be in the storefronts? What does that mean about your community? Who should benefit from the investment? In what way? How can we measure that impact?

Location focus: Do you want to impact all of downtown or main street? Is there a key block or intersection that is most important right now? Where is the energy starting to build already?

Partners at the table: Who are you already working with on downtown? Who is missing? How do you make sure that downtown or main street businesses include the diversity of your community?

Small-scale manufacturing businesses: Do you have any small-scale manufacturing businesses engaged in downtown yet? What organizations can help you find them? How will you reach diverse business owners in your community?

Real estate: Are the downtown or main street property owners at the table? Of the property owners or local developers, who really believes in the community and downtown?

Promotion and branding: What kind of public relations does the downtown have now? Is there a goal for more exposure?

Business development: Are there existing local business development programs, and if so, what are they? Who do they reach? Who do they not reach?

Land use: Does zoning in downtown or on main street allow small-scale manufacturing or artisan manufacturing as a permitted use? Does the zoning allow you to create the place you want to have?

There are more questions to answer on the worksheets. Go through them all. Think about this step as a collective brain dump, a brainstorming session, and a moment to step back and think about all of the great people and pieces you already have in your community. Without judging, throw all these ideas into a pile.

Every place has assets, even places that have been struggling for a long time. Let's be clear about that from the start. And remember that this step is just a start. You will keep adding to these lists as you interview people in step 3 (see chapter 7).

Here are a few ideas to keep in mind as you think and talk your way through these questions:

How do you want this place to feel loved and unique at the end of the process?

If you had a magic wand (stick with me on this!), and use it to create that place that is loved by you and your neighbors, what would that place feel like? (The magic wand is key. It gives people the space to think big.)

Describe the experience as you walk down the street at 4 p.m. on a Saturday. Keep this picture in mind as you work through all the pieces.

These questions may be difficult to answer, but if we don't ask them, we end up with the default outcome. And the default outcome is not inclusive, it is not unique, and it will not be resilient. These questions let us start working differently. As we answer them, we start to define what it means to be our own place. We can show that our community is important enough to us to have hard conversations and that we trust and respect one another enough to talk through these hard things.

Remember to get your copy of the Spark questions and all the details about how to go through this discussion at www.RecastYourCity.com. Make sure you have everything you need to get started.

Expect Different Answers from Different People

Here's the even tougher part: our personal backgrounds influence every way we answer these kinds of questions. That is why it is essential in step 2, find and connect with new people, to identify business and other local leaders who bring a diversity of voices into the interviews.

The pieces we work to implement end up hinging on where our answers start to overlap or diverge. Where do the different perspectives about your downtown or main street start to come together? Is there a major difference in thinking about these starting questions from different people on your starting team?

Yes, people want life back on main street. Yes, they want the storefronts filled. But who do they see in those storefronts and owning those businesses? How can that vision come together to represent the diversity of your community? How can we make those outcomes specific and achievable? Who is willing to step up and lead to make those outcomes happen? (We'll get back to this question in step 5, when we take action.)

As you can probably tell at this point, answering the Spark questions is not just a brain dump. It is about beginning the process of open conversations and talking about our community in a new way, building buy-in for action.

The technical questions—how do we fix up the storefronts, do we need to change zoning, what business development programming fits best, how can we get major anchor institutions to buy local products—will come later. Community buy-in, leadership, and new voices at the table are things you can only build from within. But the Spark discussion allows us to start that process by talking through things both big (remember that magic wand) and specific (what does it feel like walking down the street). The process starts with sitting down and talking with one another.

What This Work Looks Like on the Ground

Because our work at Recast City focuses on the overlap between downtowns, small-scale manufacturing, and strong local economies, we find that some of these answers start looking somewhat similar in different locations. That happens because in most situations, we are starting from a point of agreement that downtown or main street is important and worthy of investment and that diversity of businesses and business owners is essential. So now we ask one of my favorite questions: how can small-scale manufacturing make a difference?

To give you a sense about how these conversations play out in real life, some outcomes from a few of our project communities are given below. Your outcomes will be specific to your context, your community, and your needs, but these examples might give you a sense of where they might land.

Columbia, Missouri

You heard about Columbia, Missouri, in chapter 4: a city of about 125,000 people, with a four-lane road (The Business Loop) cutting through town about half a mile from downtown. The busy road is lined with big parking lots and vacant lots, some with a small building set back from the road, some used by car dealerships, and some sitting empty.

This stretch of the city used to be filled with local restaurants, service goods, and businesses from the community. People remember coming here with their families for a white tablecloth dinner. Now it is mostly a pass-through road filled with traffic, and few people stop along the way.

But it is also home to a city high school and the community college's advanced manufacturing technology program.

Although the properties that line The Business Loop are mostly parking lots with a few setback buildings, the areas a block or two behind that to the north and south are quite different. The south side of the corridor is bordered by a residential, fairly low-income neighborhood stretching almost to downtown that is being encroached on by student housing. The north side is squeezed between The Business Loop properties and the highway and is filled with larger urban industrial spaces that most people don't know are there: people building cabinets, working in metals and welding, and providing services for the broader region.

The Loop Community Improvement District, led by executive director Carrie Gartner and board of directors' chair Susan Hart, who owns a local construction and development company, recognized the potential of small-scale manufacturing to benefit this area, but they didn't know how to get it there or what it would look like on the corridor. Together with the rest of the board, they set out to make The Loop a place, not a pass-through.

They could have gone in many directions with their work. The board worked on talking through the core questions, and throughout the process, The Loop leadership committed to creating an inclusive business community in this area. They wanted to create a place where families come together, and they wanted to understand how people see the area. They used that magic wand to think about how to create a place where people want to gather that includes a diversity of business owners.

Through interviews and small group discussions, community members decided that they want to create a place where businesses can grow and stay, a place where local families can come for a community event or family dinner on the weekend, and a place for residents to gather (downtown is evidently "owned" by the university college students and is predominantly White-owned businesses). They wanted to create spaces for product businesses that represent the city's demographics and to purposefully create spaces and investments to support business owners of color.

It is partially a return to what was there and partially a vision to do it better. The community leaders want to make sure that Black and Latino business owners are part of this neighborhood's future development, and they recognize that these business owners are not really a part of the spaces downtown. Through the project, they came to realize that product businesses are all over the area and can be an immediate engine for growth for the corridor. They found tallow candlemakers, food-product businesses, hardware inventors from the university, and many other small producers who were sitting right there but had never been engaged by the city for space or business development support.

These clear outcomes helped to shape the rest of the project: who should be interviewed, what to look at in our analysis, and what short-term actions to recommend that will lead to this bigger outcome for the neighborhood. The vision for this diverse center of commerce helped lead to the announcement of a new commercial shared kitchen and other outcomes discussed in chapter 4.

Hoboken, New Jersey

Hoboken, New Jersey, is a tiny city (1.3 square miles and 53,500 people) across the Hudson River from Manhattan. It has an urban layout of a grid of streets and is packed with people. Most blocks are filled with three- or four-story buildings, like a really big small city's downtown.

Dawn Zimmer, then mayor of Hoboken, Brandy Forbes, Hoboken's director of planning, and other community leaders came together in 2015 to think about the quickly changing market in the city. Demand for housing was rising quickly, local residents were being priced out of apartments, and the demand was pushing industrial property owners to consider reuse of the buildings for high-end apartments.

Hoboken had something most cities just dream about: old industrial buildings with three or four floors still being used by production businesses. These buildings were home to a custom-printed wallpaper company, a musical instrument fabricator, a hardware audiovisual creation company, and so much more. But the buildings, and these tenants, were threatened by pressure to redevelop the properties into residential or office space that would draw higher lease rates.

Good-paying middle-income jobs were getting pushed out of the city, making it difficult for some households to stay. Local leaders wanted to understand how to protect some space for middle-income jobs. This conflict pushed the city to think about a question that comes up in a lot of hot markets: what is the "highest and best use" of a property?

"Highest and best use" is a phrase thrown around every city, every planning department, and any investment decision from economic development teams. It usually means "whatever we can put on this site to get the highest property value and taxes out of this property."

If that is the only priority, that is a fine definition. But instead, we suggest discussing "highest and best use" based on the outcomes we want to achieve. Does the community really need good middle-income jobs? If so, maybe the highest and best use is space for businesses that create those jobs. Does the community want to focus on ensuring affordable work space for business owners to strengthen inclusive economic development? If so, a mix of uses with an incentive for below-market-rate microstorefronts might be the best use. In all cases, we need to discuss who benefits and what outcome we are working to achieve.

The Hoboken team came together to make sure that the city's production businesses would not get displaced as the market got hotter and to understand who is here (what production businesses) and how to best support them. These priorities, and a series of interviews with small product business owners, property owners, and other civic leaders, shaped our recommendations for the city to keep these essential businesses in the community both as a way to keep middle-income jobs in town and as an avenue for more existing residents to become business owners and afford the city as it grows and changes.

Fremont, California

Kelly Kline, then chief innovation officer and director of economic development for Fremont, California, when Recast City worked with the city in 2016, recognized the lopsided nature of the city's economy. Fremont—a fairly new jurisdiction created by five suburbs coming together, with a population of almost 250,000 at the southern end of San Francisco Bay—was in the process of creating a downtown in 2016. This downtown would be the first for the city. Simultaneously, the city was getting a BART (Bay Area Rapid Transit) train station in its new innovation district, and Tesla already had five million square feet of production space in the city. Things were booming, but Kline recognized that it was uneven in a number of ways.

The city was home to some large manufacturing businesses, and it started to work with the broader Bay Area Urban Manufacturing Initiative to support this sector. Kline saw that there were many missing pieces in the city's support of manufacturing. Her team decided to focus on creating a strong pipeline of micro- and small-manufacturing businesses to take advantage of local skills coming out of large manufacturing and to diversify the businesses in the city. They did not want to be a boom-and-bust city. They did not want to have all the local jobs dependent on one megabusiness. Rather, they wanted to support and find space for more small manufacturers as they grew into stable and vibrant businesses.

In addition, the team made a commitment to find diverse business owners and pull them into the work to support this sector as a city; three-fourths of the residents are Asian, Latino, and other people of color. The city is still working to support and grow this sector today and created special tools during the COVID-19 shutdown to support diverse local businesses, including a city match for gift certificates residents bought from local small businesses.

Lafayette, Louisiana

The McComb-Veazey neighborhood of Lafayette, Louisiana, is a historically Black neighborhood near downtown. It is filled with families who have lived in the neighborhood for generations, people who ran local businesses, know one another, and help each other out. It is a place that once had its own main street, just north of downtown, but today it has too many vacant properties. The neighborhood is now predominantly low-income, with many vacant homes moving onto the city's tax lien list. In addition, the neighborhood is separated from downtown by a no-man's land corridor of property that the state owns and plans to use for a new elevated highway, a highway that will physically separate this neighborhood from the city (a legacy of racist land use decisions that are still being implemented today).

The neighborhood association called the McComb-Veazey Coterie is led by executive director Tina Bingham. She is a visionary and a make-things-happen person who works with Habitat for Humanity to bring properties off the city's tax lien list, gain control of them, and build new, affordable, single-family houses for the neighborhood so that more neighbors can buy homes. She also worked with the city and Habitat for Humanity to renovate an old house in the neighborhood and create the Community House—a center for adults and kids to come together for classes, programming, and entertainment—for the neighborhood and by the neighborhood. Bingham, alongside her mother, Trincella Bonnet, also runs a community farm to help bring healthier foods to her community and teach people how to do it.

Bingham and her team knew that there were many small-product businesses in the neighborhood but didn't know who they were or how to best support them. Their focus was to find these businesses, understand the business development needs, and figure out how to create space for these businesses in the old neighborhood main street, which was recently designated as a cultural district. They recognized the passion and energy that community members have for the businesses they created (the boudin was AMAZING!) and wanted to help them build their household wealth and build the neighborhood's economy at the same time. The team's experience working with neighbors in the community, and their commitment to the neighborhood, helped shape this outcome.

Today, Bingham is leading efforts to bring investment into neighborhood-owned product businesses and help them find space to grow. To help residents expand their food-production businesses, the neighborhood association is working on a project to launch a microcommercial shared kitchen in a shipping container, and Bingham is working on a pop-up marketplace that will promote local producers to the region. All this is being done without city funding.

What Does It All Mean?

What does it mean that these places got started, went through the Spark step, and then came up with these outcomes? It means that you can, too.

These community leaders—from inside and out local government—knew that there was so much more in their community that could help people create jobs, earn living wages, and make them proud to be a part of the community. These leaders understood that they needed to look at what was missing to build a stronger economy for their residents. They were strong enough to say what was missing and what they were going to do about it.

These leaders worked through the Spark step to understand their starting point—who do we already know, who are we missing, and why are we doing all this in the first place—because they knew that they wanted to make changes for the better. They were not complacent with what came before. They were leaders because they said, "We can do better for more people in our community."

Starting with these questions means that the team understands where it is going. These discussions are not general hand-waving, but, rather, honest conversations about who should benefit and what we want to achieve at the end. The end point is defined so that we can know if we get there.

But these conversations from the Spark questions are only the first step. We next need to find and connect with all the people.

Find All the Hidden Gems in Your Community:
Business Owners Who Make Stuff

CHAPTER 6

Step 2

Find and Connect with New People

Now that the broad outcomes, major partners, and other starting assets have been established in the Spark conversation, it is time to connect with people from the community. Through this direct and deep engagement with people in the community, we will find those who were never invited to the table, those who can help us bring new voices to the table, and those who can support taking action. This crowd will help you refine the broad outcomes from the Spark conversations into specific ones to achieve and help define how to effectively achieve them.

Direct communication and engagement—sitting and talking with the people who may be affected by the change or the investment—are critical to making sure that they are not just given a seat at the table, but are also heard. Once we understand the needs of the people in the community, we can invest in programs, support, and spaces that benefit them.

In this second step of Recast City's five-step method, we start from a completely different place than any usual groundwork for a market analysis or generic public outreach initiative. We find the right people, one by one.

As part of this step, feel free to do a cluster analysis, too, if you want. It is important to understand the economic and business data that you have in hand. But then break out of the office and talk to people, not just the usual suspects at the local chamber of commerce or the people who always show up for small-business meetings with the city or county council.

This step of finding and connecting pushes each one of us to do better. It encourages us to have in-depth conversations with different people, to get out of the office and talk to people where they are, and to ensure that the demographic diversity of the community is reflected at that table. It also gives us an opportunity to build new trust and relationships for successful economic and place development.

What is the major barrier we hear from most communities about this step? Most frequently, we hear that they don't have the time or staff capacity to do this step effectively.

Yes, this step does take time, but without it, the risk is very high that we waste more taxpayer money on programs that are not needed or not formed to best support the people and the small-scale manufacturing businesses we want downtown and as a stronger part of our economy. So think of it as a cost-saving measure.

With this step, your programs and policies are more likely to be inclusive and to succeed than if you skip this step. By speaking to people and engaging them, your programming or investments in the place will be successful faster. To achieve a stronger, more resilient local economy, a stronger downtown, and more access to wealth building for more people, you need to make sure that you are inclusive from the start. If not, the impact of your work will be subpar at best because you will be leaving a part of your community behind.

When working with clients, we spend two to three months finding people who can help us connect to the target communities, pulling names of people to interview, and analyzing who we might be missing. As a result, in the end we have a clear understanding of needs, we have community leaders with stronger relationships with people and business owners they didn't know before, and we have the buy-in to take action. The time spent to find and connect with these people is worth the investment.

Getting Started

There are four parts to this work:

1 Find the people who should benefit from investments in downtown and in business development support (including small-scale manufacturing business owners).

2 Find Connectors to the parts of your community you don't know well.

3 Find the organizations and community leaders already working in the communities affected by the project.

4 Think about who you need at the table to provide political and implementation support for the project at the start and to have buy-in at the end.

Remember that a core piece of this work is to be inclusive. We need to build all these lists to be inclusive, which means that the business owners interviewed must represent the demographics of your community. In many cases, it will mean building new relationships through introductions and new partner organizations.

Once you feel like your list is complete, check it again. Pause in your search to find and connect with all these groups, take a step back, and ask yourself honestly if the people on the list represent the diversity of your community.

Does the list represent the race, ethnicity, immigrant status, and income levels of the community? Do you have business owners on your list who represent that diversity? We need the ideas and voices of these different business owners at the table because their needs for support, and means for accessing support, may be different.

Honesty with yourself on this might be the hardest part because none of us know enough people to be able to make these lists on our own and be sure that the community is truly represented at the table. This effort takes working with lots of different people, asking lots of people for names and ideas, and getting outside—way outside—of the people we usually talk to.

From time to time throughout this process, take that step back, look critically at your lists, and ask yourself, do these people represent the larger community—or just parts of it?

To get a better understanding of this process, let's dive into the details of each part. The first is finding the right business owners.

Find the Small-Sale Manufacturing Business Owners

Small-scale manufacturing businesses, and many other types of small businesses, are not always visible to local economic development leaders. Few of these businesses are members of the local chamber of commerce, they never requested local financing, and they just have their heads down doing work. These business owners are not in one database that you can just pull off the shelf. This business sector is well-hidden because no one has taken the time to say that they are essential.

Once you start looking, you will find a treasure trove of local businesses that can fill vacant storefronts, be part of markets and festivals, and potentially scale up and create good-paying local jobs with the right business development support. But how do we find them?

The reality is that in most communities, it takes research and conversations to build a strong list of local product business owners, but you can build it incrementally and grow your list over time. The essential piece is to start the list and purposefully build it to include the racial and ethnic diversity of your community.

Below are some ideas for your search for small-scale manufacturing businesses. (One additional idea: get an intern to help if you can.)

- Google it. Do local searches for "product business," "fabricator," and "artisan."

- Pull business licensing information from the local government to find anyone under production and manufacturing. Also pull terms like "jewelry" and "machinist" to look at what businesses come up. Review a wider set of terms and find out which ones do fabrication or production onsite.

- Pull vendor lists from local festivals and farmers' markets. These lists are a wealth of information about local microbusinesses. Pull business names from different cultural events, pop-up markets, and music festivals from the past to find producers and other local businesses.

- Post a form online and ask business owners to sign up. Promote it widely and in multiple languages. Post the online form on the city's website, ask partners to share it, and work with partners to post it in community newsletters.

- Look up who is in the target neighborhood by researching the addresses and seeing who is located there (also called a reverse lookup).

- Reach out to the surrounding neighborhood (which might be residential) and find out who has a home-based business.

- Ask any business owners you meet who they know with a product business in the community.

The essential part of this process is to break out from your existing lists. Be expansive in your search. The information will only help later as you pursue other business development work.

Leaders for The Loop in Columbia, Missouri, identified small-scale manufacturing business owners from different parts of the city through online research, through personal outreach, and by asking small producers who else they knew. The Loop created an online landing page for product businesses to sign up for more information and used that same site to share new information.

The team recognized that the businesses in downtown did not reflect the demographic diversity of the community, and they wanted to do better on The Loop. They also didn't have a set group of leaders for this business sector because no one had ever reached out to producers before. These pieces meant that the engagement started from scratch, which was great.

Susan Hart, chair of The Loop's board of directors and concurrently chair of the local chamber of commerce, reached out to the new and growing Hispanic Chamber of Commerce. Hart asked the chair of the Hispanic chamber, Wadi Rodriguez, to help find producers in the community who may not be aware of the outreach that The Loop was conducting, and the chamber brought together fifteen product business owners for a discussion. This conversation was the first time that The Loop team learned about the lack of affordable space for food-production businesses. The need was something that hadn't come up in other producer interviews, but once it was an identified need, it was then echoed from many other communities in the city and became an essential part of The Loop's actions.

Find Connectors

The reality is that we know who we know, and there is no one—or at least no one I've met yet—who knows all the people in a community to effectively find all the business owners who represent a community's demographic diversity. Each person in local government or community leadership has a personal network, and it is limited. That is just the reality of human beings.

The crucial part is that we recognize this limiting factor and do something about it, and Connectors are how we get there. Connectors are an essential part of the work. They are people who are known and trusted by their community and believe in the greatness of the community and its potential. They may not have been involved in economic development or main street investments in the past, but they are seen as leaders. And yes, it is Connectors, with a capital C, because it is a leadership title to me.

Many communities have trusted leaders who just don't really believe that the place can be great again or that the community, and its people, are worthy of it. They may not say it, but it's there. The key part of finding the right Connectors is to find someone who has both the trust of their community and believes in its future.

Connectors are the people who help us find more small-scale manufacturing business owners (or other target business owners) and who help us create a diverse community of owners. Later on, they will also be able to support implementation and help reach those target populations in need.

Examples of Connectors for small-scale manufacturing often fall into the following categories (among others):

- Commercial-shared kitchen directors

- Makerspace directors

- Faith leaders

- Civic or neighborhood association leaders

- Chamber of commerce executives

Think about who is involved in the communities you are not familiar with. Look at the gaps in your research from the first part as you worked to find small-scale manufacturing business owners. Who are you missing from your community? Do the business owners represent the racial and ethnic diversity of the community? Find Connectors to help you reach those parts of your community.

The Connectors might be neighborhood-specific (if you are targeting a limited area) or sector-specific (food products). They might help across racial divides (every community has divides) or across income divides (also in every community). If home-based businesses are a key part of achieving your outcome, finding Connectors who know individuals from outside their work life will be key to bring those people together.

Be prepared to explain why you need their involvement. Many of our best Connectors have never been involved in economic development or downtown redevelopment work, but their involvement is essential. This relationship building will help your community over the long term. And bridging these divides is also the best thing to do for your community. We need to be more effective, to be faster, and work with more limited budgets, and building new relationships is how we get there.

The work to find new Connectors to reach diverse small-scale manufacturing business owners was a core element to the work in Knoxville, Tennessee. The City of Knoxville and the Knoxville Entrepreneur Center (KEC) came together to invest in and support small-scale manufacturing businesses. Madeline Rogero, then Knoxville's mayor, had announced a Mayor's Maker Council in 2016. By the time I got to work with them, the city was supporting this effort through KEC. Jim Biggs, executive director of KEC, worked with the city through a grant and support from philanthropy to add outreach and engagement for product businesses to the existing platform of the entrepreneurship organization that was helping technology businesses grow in Knoxville. With the city partnership, the organization started to hold an annual Maker's Summit to bring product business owners together to work on business development and to create a stronger network of business owners.

Through our discussion about business owners already involved, those missing from the conversation, and how to fix that, the local team realized that their outreach to find Black-owned product businesses was falling short. We worked together to identify new Connectors, and KEC reached out to the Knoxville Area Urban League (KAUL). KAUL could be a key Connector to Black product business owners because of the programming they already ran. Terrence Carter, vice president of workforce and economic development at KAUL, joined the team for discussions, and we realized that both KEC and KAUL were running startup programs for local residents. The product businesses working with KAUL were in a program for "lifestyle businesses," whereas the KEC startup program was more focused on technology-based businesses. The program leaders knew each other, but had worked in parallel, not together, because they assumed that their small businesses were different. In fact, they were both providing similar trainings to product businesses, but not bringing those business owners together to build one diverse community of small-scale manufacturing business owners.

So what changed? Everything did. KEC and KAUL came together to talk about it after the interviews and then started to bring together the product business owners through the Maker Summit and other programming. The following year, the summit featured more Black business owners in Knoxville as a major component of the event, and the team created more inclusive programming so that new programs to help small product businesses scale up now reach the diversity of business owners in the community.

Find the Organizations and Community
Leaders Already Working in the Communities

The people already working with your small-business community might overlap or be a subset of your Connectors, but they fill a different role. The organizations and community leaders we look for here are the people who can help the businesses grow, become more financially stable, and scale up where appropriate. These people are the facilitators (or the potential facilitators) of that growth.

Think about who can help your small businesses—small-scale manufacturers and others—have space to work, get more clients, create better financial stability, and potentially scale up when they are ready. All these people, and their resources, also need to be at the table.

We need to find anyone who is already working on the issue or with the target community so that we can understand what they've done and can build on their successes. And we need to find people who can help in the future.

Who are these people? Here are some suggestions:

- Commercial property owners in your target area who may partner with you on a new shared space model.

- Small-business service providers like a Small Business Development Center can provide direct technical assistance to small businesses and may be able to identify more product business owners to include in your engagement or create new programming for them.

- Community development financial institutions or community banks that make loans and provide assistance to microbusinesses can help find the businesses now and provide targeted assistance in the future.

- Start-up and scale-up programs for local businesses (that are not tech only) teach business owners (or people who have business ideas) how to launch a business and then how to make it strong and grow.

- Private investors, philanthropists, and assistance providers who focus on business owners of color and women-owned businesses in your community foundations, foundations created by major anchor businesses, or even programs out of your local government or community college.

- Anchor institutions and local government procurement leaders can lead a "buy local" initiative and lead through example to help direct more spending dollars directly into local businesses.

Don't just talk to the service providers you always talk to. Find the people who work within specific populations in your community. If you don't know who that is, ask around.

Make sure to have those downtown property owners on the list. You don't need to list all of them, but at minimum, pull the owners who have the future of your community at heart. Look for the people who believe and might be willing to do something different.

It's the same thing with the anchor institutions. Which one has leadership to do something significant for local business owners? Who is willing to really listen, talk, and maybe even try something new? Which small-business service providers get out of their office and go out to find business owners who never even knew help was available? Who is trying new things?

Our list of community leaders does not need to be every person in the space, but we do need to push ourselves to find the thinkers and doers who believe in the greatness of our community. You need to find people who are committed to building the local economy, the downtown, and even the main street storefronts to reflect the amazing demographic diversity of your community. Talk to your team, look at your target areas, think about who is already involved in these issues, and ask them for recommendations.

In Columbia, Missouri, one of the key organizations was the University of Missouri, fondly referred to as Mizzou. Mizzou owns a big, beautiful, eight-story art deco building set back behind a very large grassy front lot right along The Loop corridor. This building was vacant and possibly going to be sold off someday by the university. The Loop team brought Mizzou into the conversation because the project recognized this building as an important asset for the corridor. We didn't know at the start how we might use the building or what we might ask of the university, but we knew that this space would likely be part of the solution.

After interviews and small group meetings (coming up in chapter 6), we learned that this building housed an old cafeteria kitchen and that the city had a significant need for affordable space for food-product businesses. The Loop negotiated a lease for the empty kitchen space and launched a commercial shared kitchen, in partnership with the regional economic development board, in 2020. COVID-19 slowed the project, but the demand is so big and the connections so strong now, that the project will still move forward.

Think about Who You Need at the Table

All decisions are political. It doesn't matter if it's a new policy or program, funding commitment, or engagement strategy. So it is important to think about who needs to be at the table at the start to support this work at the end. They are people who might be in the local government, influence those decision makers, or lead significant external resources. They are people who can put their political weight behind the outcomes of this work and help make it happen.

In many communities, outreach begins and ends with this group. The reason this group is fourth on the list is that you need to find all the other groups first. Buy-in will be essential, but we need to know what to ask for—and have the crowd backing it up—to make it worth our while.

We need to think through these people at the start because we want to involve them along the way. We don't want to just reach out to them at the end with some answers. We need to brief them on this work, and we also need them to see their fingerprints on it. Do they have suggestions for people we should interview? Do they know business or property owners who should be contacted? Are there specific questions we should include in the interviews about downtown and small-business needs?

Who are these people in your community? You probably already have a number of ideas. Here are a few suggestions:

- Local elected officials

- City manager or administrator

- Directors of economic development, planning, or other local agencies

- Members of the board of the economic development authority

- Leadership at local universities or colleges

- Local philanthropists

- Formal and informal leaders of different racial and ethnic groups in the community (also possibly a Connector above)

- Procurement lead for a major anchor institution

Make sure to think about who is an ally (from your Connectors above) who is also a person who can support your work to build buy-in. Get those people involved.

Throughout this process, keep thinking about who you need to involve at the start so that you can get support and approval to implement your actions at the end. Who believes in your community and the potential of your small businesses in all their diversity?

In Columbia, Missouri, this list included the city manager, the real estate lead from the university, members of the board of the regional economic authority, the community college leaders, and the chamber of commerce. In Knoxville, Tennessee, it also included economic development staff from the city government and a group of property owners in the target area.

Each place has its own politics and its own set of people who will be open to changes and willing to support investment and actions to achieve these outcomes. Think critically about who these people are now, and then we'll make sure to include them in the interviews and small group meetings coming up in chapter 7.

What Happens Now?

After working through these steps, we have lists of people we want to engage (generally small-scale manufacturing and other small-business owners), Connectors who will help us find more of them, community leaders who support them, and people who can give us buy-in and guidance, all reflecting the diversity of people in our community.

This list-making process is hard work. It takes time. It takes resources to build this information. And if you don't get the inclusive list you need, start at the top and ask your Connectors to help you bring new people into the conversation.

You don't need a list of every small-business owner and every property owner. You need a list that can represent the community.

If you are targeting one part of downtown or a corridor, make sure to have lots of business and property owners from that area. Also pull in ones from other neighborhoods to make sure that you include all the voices you need. And if you are thinking city- or county-wide, pull people from many different neighborhoods and make sure that those people represent the diversity of your community. Not only will these new connections help with this work, but they will build your capacity for better decision making and actions in the future once you know people's needs.

If you want to use this time to create a more complete database of business owners who generally operate under the radar of community leaders, go for it. But you only need thirty to forty business owners who represent the demographic diversity of your community to move on to the next step.

The next step is conducting interviews, which is all about having conversations. Before we start, however, we need to make sure we have the right lists, and making good lists is worth the time.

Taking Action

Remember that outreach to the local Urban League or Hispanic Chamber of Commerce is not rocket science. The difference is in the action.

First, we have to acknowledge that we don't have all the relationships we need to understand what our small-business community needs, and we are done making assumptions about it and wasting time and money on programs that just don't work.

Second, we have to be willing to get out and talk to new people. We have to be willing to possibly being uncomfortable and maybe finding a great new ally. We have to be willing to ask for help and say that we don't have all the answers. We have to include new voices and find new Connectors in our community to find those voices.

Third, we need to listen. That's the part that comes next—the interviews. It's the time when we ask questions and listen really, really carefully. Are you ready?

Set Aside Time for Interviews and Listen Carefully

CHAPTER 7

Step 3

Start the Conversation and Get Great Information from Your Interviews

VICKI MILES WALKS THROUGH THE DOOR with a big smile on her face. She welcomes me into the shop and immediately starts pointing out the workspace, sewing machines, and other equipment her organization uses to teach people to sew. This shop is Sew Loved, Inc., a nonprofit organization founded in 2012 that teaches "underserved and marginalized women" and girls from South Bend to create things for themselves, learn the basics of sewing, and in some cases, learn how to operate industrial sewing machines to train for jobs in the region.

I am here for interviews with Miles and other leaders of the organization as part of our work in South Bend. The Recast City team is here to learn about what they do, how they help local product entrepreneurs, what works for them in South Bend, and what major challenges they still face.

We arrive with representatives from the city who have heard of the organization but have never visited the space. We are also joined by representatives from a local economic development organization interesting in seeing how small-scale manufacturing businesses can fit into a broader workforce development strategy for the city.

We are here to ask questions and listen. By doing so, we learned about the women and girls that Miles serves through the trainings and how these trainings successfully grew from a community volunteer program to one that provides industrial sewing training to its graduates. She shared her numbers, including how many women and girls have gone through the program, how much demand they see in the community, and how much more funding they need to expand to meet that demand.

Miles explained the barriers that these women face, including a lack of transportation options to get to the larger manufacturers without a car. If they have no way to get to a job, they can't take the job.

The space the program occupies is made available through a newly renovated space called Vested Interest launched in 2018 that offers low-cost space to incubate nonprofits and businesses and focuses on small-scale manufacturing. Vested Interest is a project of two long-time local business owners who want to give back and reinvest in the community.

The type of interview we held that day is at the core of step 3. It is all about listening, learning, and making a personal connection. It allows us to learn new things from new people and bring new perspectives into our decision-making process.

In step 2, we built a list of a strong, diverse group of people to engage in our project. Now it's time to start the interviews to understand in detail what is going on in our community and what investments are needed.

We organize the interviews in two major ways:

1 One-on-one interviews with small-scale manufacturing business owners, property owners, and Connectors who have not been engaged before in economic development or downtown discussions. Although it is one business owner talking to a few local

people, we consider it a one-on-one interview because it is all about focusing on one business owner and one business at a time.

2 Small group interviews with representatives of specific audiences, established boards of organizations, or groups providing similar support to business owners.

Both types of interviews are based on the same few core concepts, but they are conducted differently, and both are essential to the method. Thanks to the work done in the previous step of reaching out to Connectors and expanding your network, these discussions will bring out new ideas and solutions for the downtown or neighborhood.

How this process works and what we get out of these interviews is all based on the details. Let's look at the technical parts and see how each type of interview works.

One-on-One Interviews

As I mentioned, the one-on-one interview is focused on one person. It is essential that all involved in the interview give the business owner the honor and respect for that person's work and listen carefully. After the business owner answers questions, the local staff can also share ideas about how existing programs might help the business or connect the owner with others for support.

This conversation can take anywhere from thirty to forty-five minutes. The technique is based on some basic principles:

1 All interviews take place on the site of the small business (or at least the majority of them), the property being discussed, or the place of work of the Connector if they have a space.

2 A standard questionnaire is used for all interviews to collect both quantitative and qualitative information about the business or community leader, as shown in the examples below.

3 Note-taking is done on paper to make the person being interviewed feel more comfortable and to assure that person that you are not distracted by an electronic device.

4 Notes should include specific phrases (where possible) stated by the person being interviewed to describe current assets and challenges of the business, the property, or the community connections.

5 Interviews and meetings are hosted with a deadline (I do interviews and meetings over three days of ten to twelve hours each day.) You can spread them out over a month, but keep it time-bound to retain focus on the project.

The technique is specific, but for a good reason: we get really good information and build strong connections this way. Some of these steps are based on my years of community engagement, and some are pulled directly from the world of user research.

The User Research Details

Talking to people is different from interviewing them. And interviewing them is different from conducting user research. Interviewing people just means that we want to get information out of them. It doesn't give us a focused purpose, and it doesn't give us a specific method to use to get consistent kinds of information. Rather, user research gives us a specific technique with a purpose to the conversation so that we get the most useful information from a person. Doing so helps us both collect essential information about the business or Connector and build a meaningful connection with them about the outcomes we are working to achieve.

User research is a technique to understand someone's needs, behavior, and experiences. It gives us information that helps us solve target problems. We are not asking interviewees for the solutions; rather, we are learning about what works and what doesn't work for them right now in their business so we can develop solutions.[1]

User research techniques are used all the time by the tech sector to understand how a potential client will directly interact with the technology. This research reduces the risk of the investment so that no one is guessing if a specific change to an app, for example, will help people use the tool or not.

We can do the same thing with economic development investments and downtown development strategies. We can reduce the risk of the investment (will it work?) by conducting user research interviews with the target audience for the program or investment.

The discovery stage of user research is where we start in the Recast method. In this part of user research, we go to where the person works and ask them about their work and their community. We listen carefully and work to understand what is important to them.

Our goal is to understand what works and doesn't work for the business owner, but we also want to learn about business successes and constraints. Depending on the interview and where we are in our process, we can also test ideas with the person. We pull examples of policies or programs and share them with the business owner to see if that service would be useful. Are they interested in it? Does it help them address any of the barriers they brought up? We get the person being interviewed to share ideas and add to our thinking.[2]

We listen and take notes. Another goal of these interviews is to look and listen for the small pieces. How did someone react? Can we understand why they answered a question in a specific way?[3]

We put our assumptions to the side about the small-business community and talk to people directly. Although we can't talk to every business owner, property owner, and essential community Connector in a week, when we make sure to interview people from across the diversity of our community, we start with broader perspectives and broader information. The interviews give us a method to collect concrete information quickly at the start, and we keep gathering input over time as we use the same technique to talk to more people in the future.

Determining What to Ask in One-on-One Interviews

To determine what to ask in a one-on-one interview, you can create your own questionnaire or start with a template of questions from Recast City at www.RecastYourCity.com. Here are some key tips to get started.

1 Start by briefly explaining the purpose of your visit (we want to better support small business and would like your input; we want to create space for small-scale manufacturers downtown and want to understand your needs). Be specific. Share your broad goals from step 1. Let the business owner or Connector know that they are a priority in this process.

2 Ask easy, quantitative questions—size, lease space, number of employees—to get the business owner talking.

3 Ask positive qualitative questions. What works about having your business here? What assets does this neighborhood or city have that help your business? Why do you like being located here?

4 Ask critical qualitative questions. What barriers do you face? What is hard about having your business here? What needs do you have that aren't being met?

5 Ask about community and vision. Do they want to be part of a community of small businesses? Would they like to be a part of a neighborhood of businesses? Why? What could it do for their businesses? What could it do for them individually?

This flow of questions allows people to think in concrete ways, in positive ways, and then in productive critical ways about their needs. It shows that you value their input about big, tough questions.

You are not going to give them any answers at this interview except to perhaps connect them with a specific existing resource if you think it can address a gap they bring up. This time is for listening and documenting.

We are not aiming for statistical validity. We are aiming for enough input to start to see common denominators and differentiators. Some assets or challenges might come up from a bunch of different kinds of business owners. Some issues might be specific to business size or owner background or experience.

At the end of the interview, give people a sense of what comes next. People need to know how they will impact the project, what comes out at the end, and the time line. And thanking people is important. For instance, you could say: "We're interviewing people individually and in small groups over the next two weeks and then will release a set of recommendations by the end of the month. If you're interested, we'll email you updates about it along the way. We want to [state broad outcomes from step 1 here], and your feedback helps us understand how to get there. Thank you for taking the time to talk with us today."

Two examples of one-on-one interviews illustrate this method. Recast City worked with both Washington, DC, and Indianapolis, Indiana, in projects aimed at small-scale manufacturing businesses.

Washington, DC, is a city with a diverse population, a hot market, and some serious divides on who gets access to space in an expensive retail environment. I interviewed product business owners there for a regional real estate developer to understand how to bring small producers into nonprime retail space in a new construction project.

During the one-on-one interviews, I spoke with Titi Wreh, owner of Chez Kevito, who creates clothing, accessories, jewelry, and home furnishings inspired by her African roots. Wreh sells her products online and in a shared retail neighborhood storefront with other small producers. She scaled out of her home and now produces in the retail space when it is closed to the public or during quieter retail hours. Wreh talked about the barriers she faced as an immigrant opening a business, but she also talked about the welcome she received from the community for her African prints and designs for professional clothing. She spoke about her struggles to find affordable production space in the hot DC market and expand her sales reach. The shared retail space made all the difference for her because local customers could try on new products.

These details—both the things that work and the challenges to Wreh's business—informed the kinds of spaces the real estate developer considered for the mixed-use development project. The size and pricing of the space, the potential for spaces that include retail with production space behind it, and how to make it affordable to local business owners all became part of the conversation because of the input from Wreh and other local product business owners.

Indianapolis also found ways to identify small-product business owners and start to help them. The area is filled with product businesses, both in the city and throughout the region. Producers range from biotech to screen printing and from high fashion to antique car custom refurbishing. The local government, a local community development corporation (CDC), and the national nonprofit Local Initiatives Support Corporation (LISC) invested funds in a building to create shared coworking manufacturing space for producers. Although most local CDCs focus on housing, this one also focused on created space for living-wage jobs. The CDC invested in a corridor filled with vacant industrial buildings alongside a stable residential area. The industrial vacancies were starting to hurt the stability of the neighborhood, and bringing an old building back into productive use for good-paying jobs seemed like the right way to go.

The one-on-one interviews with small-scale manufacturing business owners showed a community of producers that was starting to engage.

At the time of my visit in 2015, discussions were happening about how to invest in a makerspace to grow the textile sector.

The emerging community of textile producers is known as Pattern, which is also the title of the magazine for producers in the local fashion industry. The organization's executive director, Polina Osherov, worked to make Pattern the center of the community—first through the magazine and meetups and then through a shared retail space to showcase local designers and producers.

In a one-on-one interview, it became clear that Osherov's passion for all things fashion, design, and the community may have helped inspire investment in this growing sector. Osherov laid out how the meetups grew over time, how the fashion designers worked together, and how the excitement behind the magazine showcased the designers in the region. These details helped the coalition of local government, local CDC, and LISC understand the energy and pent-up demand for textile production space and mentors. Even a little bit of support could make a big difference, both to help these businesses grow and to attract more entrepreneurs to the city.

The one-on-one interviews that you organize will reflect the excitement and potential for business growth in your community. The people you meet will share their dreams, their passions, their heartbreaks, and their worries with you. You will learn about their business and their relationships in the community. You'll engage new people and learn new things about your community. You'll talk to the doers, the people making things happen, and the people who believe in your community.

These interviews are my favorite part of every project. And it's only one part of the interview step!

Small Group Interviews

Small group interviews give you the opportunity to build relationships with a target group, learn from them, and show them that their work is important. These conversations also allow you to gauge their interest as a sector or community for future implementation. Small group interviews allow participants to quickly understand what else is going on in their sector, hear about other participants' work, and find new ways to work with one another. The groups also give you a loose coalition to go back to later to talk about how to work together on implementation.

A small group interview might include five to fifteen people from any one of these groups:

1 Property owners in the target area who believe in the future of the neighborhood

2 Small-business development service providers

3 Nonprofit organizations working with underrepresented business owners

4 Neighborhood representatives

5 Members of the economic development authority board

6 Civic leaders focused on reinvestment for the target neighborhood, such as faith leaders, community college leaders, and other service providers

7 Organizers of local farmers' markets, artisan fairs, and festivals that feature local product vendors

8 Local decision makers, such as city or county council members

9 Bankers and financial institutions

10 Improvement district or CDC board members

Each of these groups will provide different perspectives on the needs of local small businesses and their potential for growth to strengthen the community.

The small group interviews are also the prime time to reach out to home-based businesses through a trusted Connector's invitation. Most home-based business owners are not comfortable with a team coming to their homes for an interview (although I did get to see a beautiful laser cutter on someone's closed-in back porch in Vassar, Michigan, making engraved mugs for a local business). In most cases, the home-based business owner will be more comfortable meeting at a community space or at a space hosted by the trusted Connector who brought them into the conversation.

Small Group Context

Small groups of people working toward similar community goals often don't know one another or rarely sit together to talk through the sector. Small-business development service providers might know of one another, but never met to coordinate services or ensure that every part of the community is receiving support. Local bankers might meet to talk about residential investments, but never participated in a conversation about microloans and the gaps in the local financing sector.

The information you get out of the small group interview will complement and provide broader context for some of the information you get out of the one-on-one interviews. For instance, if a small-product business owner talks about the need for mentors in a particular sector, the small group interview with small-business service providers can clarify whether or not there is a mentorship program or if there is a communication gap between service providers and those in need (a challenge that comes up in many communities).

Small group interviews are similar in structure to one-on-one interviews, but because of the general nature of group conversations, they don't delve as deeply into each person's "why." Small group conversations often work best at this stage with people from common industries or roles in the community.

The goal of these discussions is to give people an opportunity to share their vision for the potential of small businesses in the target area, talk about ways they can help and gaps they struggle with, and get the people in the group to connect with one another over this shared vision. It is also an opportunity to share your goals with the group. Where are you all going with this work? How can they work together to help achieve it? What role can they serve to help implement the work?

In a small group environment, the interview structure and method differ from one-on-one interviews a bit. In a small group meeting, it is the responsibility of the facilitator to make sure that each participant has the opportunity to share. You can go around the table for each question and ask each person to respond for the most important questions, or you can ask for volunteers and then gently invite quieter participants to share their thoughts. But remember that facilitation of these conversations is critical to make sure that everyone's voice is heard.

It will be up to you to determine how many small group interviews will be essential to getting a complete picture of both what is going on right now and the buy-in you need for implementation. Remember the groups of people we identified in chapter 6? Those people need to be part of small group interviews to ensure that you have a complete picture that represents your community and has the buy-in and support for implementation at the end.

Also remember to make sure that the interviews represent the community's diversity. The purpose of that work in chapter 6 was not just to have that diversity on the list, but to ensure that those views are reflected in the information collected from the interviews as well.

Determining What to Ask in Small Group Meetings

The interview questions for small groups overlap with those used for one-on-one interviews. You can get the template of questions at www .RecastYourCity.com, but feel free to create your own questions for these small groups.

Here are some points to consider:

1 Start by explaining your purpose, without using technical terms. Why are we bringing this group of people together? What are you trying to achieve? The "whys" should come from the broad outcomes you established in the Spark step. What do you want to see happen at the end of this process? Share this thought with the group. Do you have a local decision maker participating in the small group meeting? Ask that person to briefly talk about their "why" for the initiative. An explanation from a local leader is a strong motivator for discussion because people see the potential for action at the end.

2 Get people to start talking by asking them about their vision. Now is the time to employ your magic wand. If you could see what this street, neighborhood, or downtown would look like after all our work, what would you see as you walk down the street? This question gets people thinking big, positive thoughts and helps people understand in their own words why they are thinking about these issues. It gets them to recognize the potential.

3 Next ask people to share the community's assets that can benefit local small businesses. We always want people to think about positive attributes before addressing challenges. The asset might be a program they offer or something they recognize in the community. The assets can be anything, from people volunteering a lot to great transit or from beautiful storefronts to a really interesting diversity of business owners. Push people to think big, positive thoughts about the community, even if it's struggling.

4 Then ask people to share the challenges. What is hard about having a small business here? What are the barriers?

5 Finally, ask them for their ideas about what to do. Do they know of any examples from other communities that could make a difference?

Make sure to document it all it as you go, taking notes as you did with the one-on-one interviews.

In Columbia, Missouri, as previously discussed, the Business Loop Improvement District north of downtown has a four-lane road and parking lots everywhere. The group of property owners who created the district knew that it could be so much more. The Loop's board of directors was filled with these property owners, who felt like they had nothing to lose and a lot of potential to achieve. When we worked with them to interview small groups, we met with more than a dozen different groups, including small-business support organizations, the regional economic development authority, bankers, property owners, Hispanic Chamber of Commerce members, graduates of the advanced manufacturing program at the community college, and Black business owners with home-based businesses. These group interviews complemented our one-on-one interviews with product businesses owners who made tallow candles, clothing, food products, hardware, jewelry, and so much more.

Our small group interview with members of the Hispanic Chamber of Commerce was an essential step. These business owners were not involved in the primary board of the local chamber. Their voices were not on the regional economic development authority's board. When we met with these business owners, we quickly learned that the people who had food businesses struggled to find affordable and available space for production. We also learned that they were not aware of the existing business development support available in the city and that it may not serve some of their needs because programming was only offered in English.

This information echoed what we had heard in some of the one-on-one interviews. People had food businesses at home or in borrowed spaces and couldn't grow because of limited capacity. They didn't have any support for food businesses and didn't know where to turn for mentors, investment, or any other kind of help. After about eight small group interviews with different local groups, the need was clear from across the community of established chefs, immigrants, and Black business owners: food-product businesses were stifled because of this lack of space and lack of support.

It is this magic combination of one-on-one interviews and small group meetings that gives us the details we need to understand what is going on with the small businesses in our community. With this information, we can determine what we need to do next.

How to Make It Stick

These interviews and small group meetings are gold. I don't know how else to describe them. They give us a chance to learn from people about parts of our community that we never knew about. The meetings allow us to meet new people and get out of our old routine. And the meetings—especially when they can be done onsite, with visits to the production businesses—create an opportunity to see the amazing work of our own local business owners.

These meetings and interviews can be the start of new relationships that change the way you see your community and change the way you lead engagement for local projects. The people you meet and the connections you build are a new kind of asset for your community.

Bringing these people to the table, visiting their spaces to show that they are essential to the economy, and keeping them involved are all part of the long-term benefits of this work. Three last points about this work should be emphasized, however, before we move on to talk about how to understand all this amazing raw information from the interviews.

Talk to the Believers

In many communities, there are legacy property owners. They are people who bought properties in the 1960s or 1970s or received it as it passed through generational hands. Many of these owners have no interest in investing in the place or the property anymore. They are happy to either take it as a loss or just get a small revenue out of whomever is willing to use the space as it slowly deteriorates.

These property owners may end up being key to our downtown work, but we don't start out by trying to convince the skeptics. In the end, though, we may come up with a set of actions to address this barrier to downtown reinvestment. Can we help them sell some properties that someone else can redevelop to be part of their legacy? Can we get them to partner with a local business to try something new? All these kinds of questions can come out in the discussions and analysis. But before talking to the skeptics, let's first talk to the believers, the people who truly believe in downtown and the community's potential. Let's find out what they think about the great potential of the place and the people there.

Stay in Touch

After all the one-on-one interviews and small group meetings, we end up with a ton of information, which we talk about in chapter 8. We also end up with a crowd of new relationships, ones that will be essential to implement our ideas at the end, that will help you understand what is really needed over the long-term, and that you can bring to the table to ensure that new programs and policies truly do benefit all your small businesses.

So make sure to have a simple plan to keep up with all those new friends. An email list is the easiest way to do it. But also make sure to keep that conversation going over time. It will be worth it.

Remember to Build Buy-In

Some of the people we identified in chapter 6 are the ones essential for buy-in to make things happen at the end. The interviews and small group meetings are when we meet with them. In the process, though, remember to look for potential champions for implementation; those people are probably worthy of one-on-one meetings. Also meet with the full economic development authority, city or county council, or any other major influential group that needs to "buy in" to this concept and see how it helps their work, too.

All these people need the opportunity to see and hear about the potential of this work, understand the opportunity and urgency around it, and see how it benefits their own goals for the community. We often need to be able to pass policies, get investment, or create new programs at the end of this work. We need the buy-in and political will to do it. Now is when that step starts.

Interviews with business owners, property owners, Connectors, and small group meetings with key audiences who can make a difference for buy-in and implementation in the end are all parts of this interview step. It means that you have an opportunity to build new relationships and learn new information at every meeting. It also means that you lower the risk of any investment informed by these interviews because the investment is based on the need you identified with the people in the community. These interviews and meetings allow the community to be more targeted with each dollar spent and more successful in its support for small businesses to grow a stronger, more inclusive local economy.

Now we need to understand what all the interviews mean. Then we can pull all the steps together to create a great place with thriving businesses.

Look for the Projects: A Commercial Shared Kitchen
Can Help Product Businesses Grow

CHAPTER 8

Step 4

Analyze the Input and Understand What It All Means

AFTER INPUT IS COLLECTED FROM INTERVIEWS AND small group meetings, we analyze it and identify what is already amazing and works for our community (assets) and what is still missing and is most needed by our business owners (gaps). The goal of this step in Recast City's five-step method is to understand the issues that came up frequently with everyone or issues that came up frequently for specific populations. We need to understand these differences to help us achieve the goals and intentions we set out at the start. We also want to think about what comes through clearly from the discussions, as well as what people might not say explicitly because it was the first time meeting. Look for those gaps.

Understanding what it all means requires us to think openly and be ready to hear things about our community that we didn't know or didn't recognize before. By doing so, we make changes that make a difference.

Where It All Starts

In this fourth step, we begin by reviewing the broad outcomes from step 1 and reminding us of our priorities. The interviews generally produce an overwhelming amount of information, but the details we want to analyze are the ones around our outcomes and the urgency we identified at the start.

First, think about your goals. Does your community have a priority around affordable space for small businesses on main street? If so, pay close attention to comments around cost and square footage. Does your community have a goal of assuring that main street is diverse? If so, look closely across racial and ethnic populations to see who has access to downtown space. Does your community have a goal of keeping businesses that want to scale up? If so, look at how people describe their ambitions to grow and what kind of support they need.

Second, review the interviews and meetings for what went unsaid. Consider that you may have just started to build trust with the people you interviewed. Maybe you knew some of the people well but others not very well, if at all, before the interview. Because many of the people you interviewed probably haven't been involved in this kind of process before, they don't know how—or if—you will follow through with this conversation or even understand clearly how you will use this information. All this building of trust (or lack of it historically) might mean that in your conversations they have explained some things directly but only inferred or hinted at others.

In one community, some small-business owners raved about the startup business development program, while others knew it existed but didn't feel like it was for them. Why didn't they think the startup program was for them? Is the location too far from where they live and has no bus access? Or is the division based on race or ethnicity? Many times, people feel more comfortable if a program is offered in their neighborhood or by people who look like them. These points may not be stated outright, but might be suggested in some way through the interview.

Look also for differences in experiences across your community. Is there a difference in access to space or support between people who already have a long-standing business in the community versus someone new to the community? Is there a difference across income lines? Is there a difference across languages or histories? Listen carefully and review your notes to see what wasn't said.

Finally, leave the rest of the information on the cutting room floor. Although this step is hard, there will be a lot of feedback about things that are not on your priority outcomes list. Compile this information and share it with local agencies or partners; you can act on those issues later. For now, our goal here is to stay focused and implement our priorities. Our goal is to save downtown with small-scale manufacturing.

Reviewing the feedback is a bit of an artform itself. The more you do it, the easier it gets. Through this process, you will see what is there and notice what might be missing.

General Questions about the Input

Here are some questions to consider as you review the feedback from the interviews and meetings in general.

1 What community assets did business and property owners mention again and again?

2 What are people proud of when they talk about the target neighborhood? How does that make them feel?

3 Did different assets come up when you spoke to business owners versus other community leaders?

4 Are there different assets across racial, ethnic, income, and gender lines?

5 What was common about the way people envisioned the area using the magic wand?

6 What challenges came up for business owners versus community leaders?

7 How are the challenges perceived by bankers, investors, and economic development leaders different from those mentioned by small-business owners and property owners?

8 What wasn't said? Is there some glaring and obvious issue in the community that no one brought up? If so, why?

9 Are there small challenges that could make a really big difference for the businesses?

Use these questions to make a longer list of the assets and challenges brought up by the people you interviewed. Look at which ideas support or create challenges for the broad outcomes you identified in the first step (the Spark) and make a short list of them. Hold the rest of the assets and challenges to the side for now.

Detailed Review Using Eight Elements of Success

After we review the input broadly, we use the Recast City framework of eight major elements that are essential to building a strong place with strong local businesses to examine the details of what might be missing. These elements are based on the questions asked in chapter 5 when we lit the Spark. We used these elements to understand who and what assets we have for the project and the context, outcome, and urgency to make it happen.

The elements are clear outcomes, location focus, partners at the table, business identified, real estate buy-in, land use policy, promotion and branding, and mentorship and scaling. I created these eight elements at Recast City over decades of working with different communities across the United States, from big to small and urban to rural. What I've found is that the community is much more likely to succeed in creating a great place with strong local businesses when these elements are part of the solution.

By reviewing the feedback for these eight elements now, you can go back and get more information if necessary. Below, we discuss what each of the eight elements means, explain how to understand information about it from the interviews, and share examples of how places took

Eight Elements of Success

on that topic. Then, when we get to the action step (chapter 9), we will be able to review each element for potential actions in support of our outcomes. There are many options in each element for action, so making sure that we have enough information on each one now helps set us up for clear answers and actions next.

 ## 1. Clear Outcomes

Review the intentions you established in the Spark and refine them as needed based on input from the interviews and small groups. If the outcomes that the community wants to achieve are not clear, focused, and measurable (maybe you left them a bit squishy at the beginning), now is the time to go back and clarify them. You need clear goals so that when you implement your plan you can show success. Although this step might feel rather risky because you are putting it out there for anyone to see if this works, it's the only way we'll know if we get there.

Fremont, California, had a clear set of outcomes for its project. Kelly Kline, the city's economic development director, knew that the city needed to build up its pipeline of small-scale manufacturing businesses and not be completely dependent on one major manufacturer for the economic future of the city (Tesla has five million square feet of production space in Fremont). She asked us to help identify the pipeline of small and growing producers, recommend programs to help them, and then determine a way to integrate the consumer facing businesses into the new downtown being built in the city.

Tina Bingham in the McComb-Veazey neighborhood of Lafayette, Louisiana, knew that her neighborhood needed to create its own economic engine and its own center for the community to come together. She recognized the potential of product businesses to help reach these goals. Bingham set her goal to bring the home-based product businesses out into the light, get them business support, and find a way to start rebuilding (and reowning) a neighborhood main street for the community and by the community.

2. Location Focus

Think about how and where these small businesses will best thrive in your community. Check back on your first thinking in the Spark. Are you focused on one neighborhood or the community's Main Street? Are you looking city- or countywide at multiple downtowns? How can you use this effort to create an epicenter for this small-business sector? How can a focus on one or two specific locations in your community help achieve your outcomes?

Maybe you learned in the interviews that the area with the most need or the best opportunity to change in the short term is a subsection of downtown. If so, focus specifically on that area now. Make sure that you have some limited geography defined for implementation.

I often work with communities that focus on downtown, Main Street, or a neighborhood center. (Small-scale manufacturing businesses—especially consumer product ones—love being in storefronts on Main Street.) Did you choose to focus on an old industrial area or a long, neglected corridor near downtown? That's also a good choice. Are you a county and need to see impact more broadly? If so, pick a few neighborhood centers, but pick something, pick somewhere. That way, you can see the impact of your work in a shorter amount of time, and others can see it, too. A focused area lets us make change happen faster.

Fairfax County, Virginia, with more than one million people just west of Washington, DC, wanted to make sure that the entire county would be more welcoming to small-scale manufacturing. The county decided to focus on how to reuse vacant commercial space, both to fill the vacant spaces in the market and to find low-cost leasable space for these businesses. But implementation at the county level would take too long, and the needs of the business owners might differ in the forty-one municipalities that make up the county. One decision we made was to focus on interviewing business owners from a limited number of municipalities but that represent different histories and different populations. That way, we could understand both the needs of these product business owners and also understand any barriers to implementation that might be different in various parts of the county. In the end, we learned that demand for affordable small-scale manufacturing space was high and that business owners from all over the county felt welcomed but all struggled to find space—from industrial areas to storefronts.

Grants Pass, Oregon, knew its target location from the start—it was all about downtown. City leadership from the planning department understood that downtown needed to be stronger and to do that, it needed more—and a greater variety of—businesses downtown. The area included the historic downtown, which is only a few blocks long, and a growing part of downtown closer to the Rouge River. All our questions and interviews focused on how to get product businesses downtown and the barriers to that outcome. Our geographic focus helped the team focus on zoning and permitting issues specific to downtown that were barriers to small-scale manufacturing business growth, as well as other needs like consistent store hours and downtown programming to bring people together.

 ### 3. Partners at the Table

Check out the partners you brought to the table in chapters 5 and 6. Are they the right people? Are you missing someone key to support your implementation at the end? Do the people at the interview and small group meeting tables represent the demographic diversity of your community? Are there people involved who have the power (funding, property, or influence) to act on the ideas at the end?

If you are missing someone or had a hard time getting your community Connectors to bring target populations to the table, now is the time to go back and get them. Ask for help. Meet with people on their home turf or on the Connector's home turf. Ask someone who knows that community to extend the invitation for you. Think about how to get the people and the information you need now.

In Columbia, Missouri, The Loop leaders recognized that the existing organizations and coalitions of small-business owners in the city did not represent the demographic diversity of the city. Black and Latino business owners did not have a seat at the table for most citywide business discussions. The downtown businesses, the economic development authority, and the chamber of commerce were predominantly White, while the city's demographics show that at least one-fourth of its population is Black, Latino, or other people of color. The leaders of The Loop worked through their own networks—people they had met in the community over the years—and then used their leadership role in the city to pursue their own one-on-one conversations with Black and Latino business owners to bring them into the conversations.

That investment of time helped the team build partnerships that brought different business owners into small-group discussions and informed the outcome of the project greatly. This input helped The Loop see that investing in a commercial shared kitchen was an essential resource for diverse business owners to thrive. This engagement also helped The Loop begin to build relationships with the first food-product business owners they would invite to work in the space, working to make sure that the inaugural cohort in the kitchen would specifically focus on Black and Latino business owners.

The McComb-Veazey neighborhood had a key partnership already at the table to help out with implementation: the local chapter of Habitat for Humanity. Bingham already worked with that organization to build new single-family houses and renovate an older house to become a community house for the neighborhood. This partnership already crossed from residential-only work (often the case with Habitat for Humanity projects) to community space. The project helped the local team see that they could expand their partnership to focus on main street next. The obvious next question was, how do we help you continue to build that work and start to build and renovate commercial space for the neighborhood businesses? This partnership wasn't new, but this long-term relationship could be part of a new solution.

 4. Businesses Identified

Take a look at the businesses you identified for the interviews and those owners who came to the table to talk with you. Do they represent the demographic diversity of your community? How can you achieve that if you didn't get there yet? Which one of your Connectors can help you reach a few more business owners from the populations that you didn't reach yet?

Then think about how you will keep growing this list. Do you have a way to keep collecting information about small businesses? When we work with communities to identify small-scale manufacturing businesses, one of the first needs is some way to collect and compile this new information. An online form and a database are an easy place to start. Online mapping with a database is a step further. Although those are potential implementation steps, now is the time to think about how you will continue to identify and collect more business information as you move forward.

Columbia, Missouri, pursued that direct relationship building through personal outreach and also created a website to promote the work and continue to collect information about local producers who would be interested in getting involved in The Loop.[1] To start collecting business names, the local team launched a website in a matter of days. They then used that website to promote public events and artisan markets, and they made it a part of the broader brand of The Loop.

Knoxville, Tennessee, created an online directory of the local product businesses. The site is hosted by the Mayor's Maker Council and run by the Knoxville Entrepreneur Center. It gives product businesses an online destination to join local business development activities and gives customers a way to look through and buy from these businesses. The site is called TheMakerCity.org, claiming the mantel of being "the" city for maker businesses.

 ### 5. Real Estate Buy-In

Review your interviews and small group meetings to see what kind of representation you have from the real estate community. Do you have property owners at the table who are forward-looking and believe in your community? Do you have developers in the region who can help implement a big (or small) idea? Are there small, local, incremental developers who can take on one storefront at a time and make a big difference?

We need real estate buy-in to make our work happen on the ground. Property owners can support our work to achieve the goals we lay out. As a first step, however, we need to make sure that we have a few property owners who believe in the outcomes we are working to achieve and who believe in the community. If you're missing these people (make sure you have at least one or two of them), go back and find them. Alternatively, find people who believe in your community who can become those property owners or incremental developers. You might find people who own successful businesses in the area who believe in your downtown or in the target neighborhood and could become small-scale developers or people from the neighborhood who believe in it and with the right support could invest in storefronts and renovations. These people can become your main street owners. Be sure they are at the table.

One of the key property owners might be the local government. In Knoxville, the city owned a small but key property on the main street of our target neighborhood. This property was near the area where other small-scale manufacturing businesses were already starting to colocate, close to the community college that could take a leadership role in entrepreneurship training, and in the middle of an area of mostly vacant and underused buildings. In the interviews, we talked to private-sector property owners, but we were also clear with the city that its property could be the catalyst for the neighborhood and used as a space to test how to bring microbusinesses together under one roof.

In McComb-Veazey, the real estate buy-in is mostly about gaining control over a few properties. Some current property owners along the neighborhood main street are not very interested in investing in their properties or are not interested in creating spaces for neighborhood businesses. So our focus on real estate buy-in was more about how to continue to partner with Habitat for Humanity to gain control of adjudicated commercial properties. The neighborhood could use the same model for commercial property as is used for new single-family houses built with Habitat and could build space for local businesses and small-scale manufacturers from the neighborhood. This way, they could start to control more of their own future to build the main street that the neighborhood residents want to see come to life.

 *6. Land Use*

Examine the land use policies in your target area. What assets and challenges came up in the conversation that might be in conflict with the zoning and permitting? What might be permitted but in conflict with the outcomes?

It's not just that we support the small businesses. Where they go matters. The magic happens when we work from the start to see where investing in business comes together with investing in a location.

In the case of small-scale manufacturing, zoning often prevents production from happening in the storefronts. It can be an easy fix (although it needs leadership and political buy-in), but one that we need to recognize and act on (in the next step).

Did zoning and permitting policies come up as gaps or barriers in the interviews? Is there a perception of a barrier versus what is actually in the policy, a perception that could be internal to the jurisdiction's staff or external with the property or business owners? Now is the time to see what land use policies might be helpful to achieve the outcomes in the target area.

Columbia, Missouri, updated its zoning code before our project there in 2019 and designated The Loop as a mixed-use area. The new code gives property owners on the corridor the option of building multistory structures with ground-floor commercial space and offices or apartments above it. But the market wasn't there. New mixed-use construction would not pencil out in the current market of the city and on The Loop. The cost of construction versus the price per square foot to lease a space didn't make any sense. In addition, new construction commercial space in a mixed-use project would be outside the price range of any local small-scale manufacturing business. And last but not least, the mixed-use zone allowed a lot of uses, but not small-scale manufacturing.

We brought these issues into the discussions about assets and barriers to achieving the outcomes we set out at the start: bring The Loop to life as a place for businesses and families with small-scale manufacturing. As a result, we worked with local leaders to draft overlay zoning language that would allow artisan manufacturing as a permitted land use along The Loop. We also worked with local developers to identify low-cost prefab construction models that would be affordable to the small-scale manufacturing businesses they wanted in the district and be a design asset to the neighborhood. The short-term answer would not be mixed-use, multifloor buildings, but the prefab option could activate the district and allow the community to start making a place where people want to come together even now.

Fairfax County, Virginia, wanted to change the zoning even more comprehensively. The county was in the middle of a major zoning rewrite, but knew that it needed to make short-term changes along the way to help the struggling office market. We worked with county staff to draft an amendment for a new artisan manufacturing land use definition so that businesses could use vacant commercial spaces as quickly as possible. We also worked with the permitting team—health, fire, and all the other pieces—to test how the approval process would work. We created three scenarios to show how an existing building could be used by one or many product businesses, and we started to work through all the questions to understand how that use in that building could be approved. Although it wasn't easy, it was an essential step to make the land use change work. Within six months, the county had passed the land use amendment.

 7. Promotion and Branding

As you look at the assets and gaps from your interviews, look at the broader system around the neighborhood or target area of your work. Does it have a brand? Does anyone promote this area in a purposeful way? Is there programming that takes place in that area?

We know from extensive work by major national real estate developers that promotion of an area through events and programming can make a world of difference regarding how people perceive an area and whether or not they want to spend time there. They need to see themselves as a part of that area.

Is there no branding and no programming? Did people in the interviews and small group meetings talk about people not knowing about the area, or did they talk about the perception of the area and having a hard time attracting people? Maybe the area is the best-kept secret, which in itself might be fine. Many downtown development authorities and main street programs spend a lot of time on programming but may not have invested time in other elements of this list. You might be completely set on branding, but be sure to think about your outcome and whether or not something might be missing. Note that this element is lower on the list because you need to work on the other ones first. A brand doesn't do anything for you unless you have a way to build on it.

Columbia, Missouri, created an entirely new website during the project and then even rebranded and launched a newer one in 2020, Cre8como.com, to strongly promote the idea for The Loop. The local team used this site to announce projects, promote events, and talk about artisan markets they created to start bringing the community together with local producers in the target area. The team also used this site to continue to get local producers to join a registry and to give them quick access to resources and support. It is a one-stop shop that helps any business owner in the region, but it focuses on the actions taking place on The Loop. As the effort grew, the team also added a space to the site that helps business owners find space on The Loop and helps property owners build there too. They baked this brand and identity back into The Loop's website, too. Makers, small-scale manufacturing, and the diversity of the community all became core parts of the identity of the place.[2]

Baltimore, Maryland, took on branding even before we had the opportunity to work with the community of producers there. In this case, the brand isn't for a location, but for the business sector itself. The Made in Baltimore brand was an outgrowth of a federal Economic Development Administration grant in partnership with the city government to find and promote small-scale manufacturers in the city. The program launched a Made in Baltimore certification for manufacturers, makerspaces, shared production spaces, and retailers that feature local small-scale manufacturers. MadeinBaltimore.org became the flagship of an organizing entity working to bring the diversity of business owners to one really big table and promote it throughout the city and the region.

8. Mentorship and Scaling

Review how the business owners talk about business development support in the community. In the interviews, did people know where to access help? Do they feel comfortable accessing what is there? Did you find out from the small group meetings with the business support network if there is startup training and programming for businesses that want to grow? Is there an established method for business owners, from every diverse population in your community, to access mentors who are knowledgeable about their sector? Do business owners from different racial, ethnic, and educational backgrounds each have access to, and feel comfortable with, available training?

Every business needs help. For example, there's an entire system of help for tech startups: startup trainings, accelerators, mentors, investors. Books have been written all about ways to create and scale up these businesses.[3] Rarely, though, is all this knowledge applied to other business sectors.

You shouldn't expect to have all the pieces. There is a continuum of small-business support, and only a few rare (and large) places have programs for all the business needs. Helping people understand how to start and launch a business, how to take a microbusiness and make it more profitable, and how to scale up a small business to be larger and stable are all parts of the continuum. Take a look at what you are missing. Are these gaps that impact the outcomes you established in the Spark stage? Which ones are the most essential for your outcomes? Add them to your barriers and gaps list. Which ones do you have (recognizing that you might not be reaching all the business owners in need)? Add them to your assets list; we'll build on them.

In Cincinnati, Ohio, we interviewed artisan business owners to understand if there was a gap in affordable workspace for this sector and what kind of support these businesses needed to thrive. When we interviewed business owners, some said that they found mentors through personal relationships in the community, and others said that they were working on their own. We also spoke with the people at the tech accelerator, The Brandery, that was in the process of launching and quickly understood that this space would not include product businesses. One existing program, First Batch, led by Matt Anthony, was leading the way and helping small producers go from prototype to production, however. This program helped business owners refine their initial model and then connected them with regional manufacturers for scalable production. But there was no broader startup training or mentorship available to small-scale manufacturers and no programming like in the tech sector to help product businesses grow. These issues became clear gaps in achieving the outcome that needed to be addressed in local actions.

Columbia, Missouri, also heard from small producers that they needed help. The food-product businesses were each finding their way on their own and didn't have any business development support. In addition, some of the business owners of color didn't feel as if the startup training available in downtown was really for them. We recommended that The Loop locate business training programming on the corridor and invite people from the surrounding neighborhoods to take part and feel ownership of the new program. It could build on the assets of the program downtown. More importantly, a new location could make a big difference in who felt like they belonged. Ultimately, The Loop decided to integrate the startup training and mentorship support into the commercial shared kitchen launched in 2020.

Step Back and Breathe

Regardless of where you are or how amazing your community is about local investment, you will find a lot of gaps. If you aren't finding gaps, you aren't being honest with yourself and your community. In fact, you might find an overwhelming number of gaps, which is fine. These gaps point you to other great actions to pursue.

The goal here is to understand what is really going on in your community and, ideally, in your target neighborhood. It is the moment to take an honest look at what works and who benefits from it, not in general, but in the specific. Don't gloss over the details to talk about the intent of programs.

Often, local programs skip this step because they are afraid of what they might see. It doesn't matter if it is a program from the local government, a nonprofit organization, or the philanthropic community—we are scared to see if all our work in the past is as effective as we've been selling it.

Think about it as a business. If a business is not reaching a specific outcome through its work (revenue, impact, community benefit), the owner changes the plan if they want to stay in business. We need to hold our programs and policies to the same standard based on the outcomes we set at the start.

Now that you have your laundry list of assets and gaps, step back and look at which ones contribute to achieving your outcomes and which ones create barriers to the outcomes you set out at the start. Look at which ones are your best assets and build on those to help achieve these outcomes. You have many of them. Think about which ones can make the biggest difference. We build on our strengths. When looking at barriers, don't take on all the gaps at once. Focus on the ones that directly impact your target outcomes—the people and the place that should benefit from this work first. Keep the rest for another conversation.

In the end, you will have limited resources (time, money, political will) to invest in big changes. For the best success, we want to find small, short-term opportunities to build on our assets and get there faster.

Now you're ready to act. You have the outcomes, the place, the partners, and all these other pieces in hand. You have a clear sense of your priorities both to build on your strongest assets and to fix your most important gaps in the way of achieving your outcomes. Now let's get ready to make stuff happen.

Take Action to Create Great Places for Everyone

CHAPTER 9

Step 5

Be Impatient and Act Now

You have all the parts. Now it is time to act. Now is also the time to be impatient.

Too often, work in economic development or planning means long plans that take three to five or more years to come to life. Instead, at this final stage of Recast City's five-step method, you should pick three items that you can act on in the next three months. Limiting our focus to items on which you can immediately act means that people will see our project and be able to build on it.

Here are a few reasons it is important to focus on these immediate actions:

1 People need to see short-term wins to believe that bigger things are possible.

2 Small wins will build political will for larger initiatives.

3 You will build momentum every time you take action and implement something, just like exercising a muscle.

For example, you may be able to amend zoning to include artisan manufacturing as a permitted land use within a matter of months, launch a website to promote and connect producers, or even expand a startup or scaling program to include producers. These smaller, quick projects will help you prove the need for larger investments and help achieve bigger initiatives that can make a major difference to your entire economy over the long term.

You can also act on changes that might take a bit longer—even up to twelve months—but be sure that you communicate with the community frequently along the way to show progress. Those wins along the way are essential to start helping your community immediately and to prove that this work has meaning, has political support, and can succeed.

Remember that the intention of this work is to help you make great places in your community. You are not aiming to make a great plan, but to actually make a great place. All the short-term steps are about action, and they all build toward major longer-term change to create inclusive, strong, local economies.

From now on, there's no more talking about local needs without change. There's also no more leaving people and places behind.

Changing Downtown and Small-Scale Manufacturing for Good

The examples in this book provide a glimpse into what is happening in places working hard to make sure that their small-scale manufacturing business community gets stronger, has space to grow, and is inclusive. Local leaders all over the United States are making these things happen in their own community in small and really big ways.

Although the actions you choose to pursue will be specific to your community and your outcomes, a few examples stand out. Consider these models as ways to think about taking a big jump forward if these policies, programs, and projects respond to a gap you identify from your interview analysis.

Make Local Procurement from Anchor Institutions a Reality

Big, long-term projects might include, for example, changing the way a jurisdiction makes investment decisions through its procurement decisions. Are any of those dollars going to local small-scale manufacturers? Every time the jurisdiction or an anchor institution (hospital, college, big business somewhere in the region) spends money on its supply chain, it could choose to spend those dollars to support local businesses and reinvest in the community, too.

Many local institutions, from schools and colleges to local government and major businesses, procure many of their products from far away. In our work, we can assess what products can be procured from local or regional businesses and help support businesses that produce essential needs during nonemergency times. Local anchors can make procurement commitments to the community, as with Johns Hopkins University in Baltimore and its Hopkins Local program, which spent $113 million with local vendors over its first three years.[1] The economic development partner can also host pitch competitions or speed-dating events for the small producers where the anchor institutions present their product needs or challenges they face and invite local business owners to fulfill those needs.[2]

This work often means that one person meets with an anchor institution, works with them to identify specific products (or services) that they could procure locally, and then leads outreach to local small businesses to make the introduction and share technical information with those producers so that they can successfully bid on the work. It takes this kind of detailed work to get started, but it can mean millions of dollars spent (invested) in local businesses. At the start, you may get anchor institutions to procure a few items from the local market, but by publicly supporting this sector and presenting the product needs annually, the sector will grow—and so will your economy. The local government can lead the way by explicitly establishing a local procurement commitment and working to bring producers and service providers into the light.

Invest Purposefully in Space for Business Growth

The real estate space needs of small-scale manufacturing businesses will almost always be an issue. You may be able to respond to a few of these needs in the short term with pop-up space, vendor events, and online markets, but some will take a while to figure out. We need to ensure that small spaces suitable for small-scale manufacturing exist in the community. (Remember that most product businesses employ fewer than twenty people, and often fewer than five.) These businesses often need industrial-priced space (versus retail prices) and less than 1,000 square feet of floor space.

These businesses can occupy vacant storefronts, as discussed in earlier chapters, but there are also a number of other models across the country that create space for small-scale manufacturers. The local community development financial institution (CDFI), Bridgeway Capital, in Pittsburgh, Pennsylvania, recognized that the local product businesses it supported through loans did not have an affordable place that would allow these businesses to have safe space and grow. At the same time, the organization recognized that keeping good-paying jobs in Homewood, one of the target neighborhoods, would be essential for neighborhood residents to build wealth for their families. To help address these challenges, Bridgeway Capital became a nonprofit developer in 2013 and began to redevelop a major industrial property, 7800 Susquehanna, in the center of the community. This property provides affordable space to neighborhood product businesses alongside nonprofit organizations, job training programs, and other small businesses. Today, it is an anchor for the neighborhood and a core asset for small businesses in the area. The once vacant building is home to businesses employing one hundred people and growing.

Examples of properties like 7800 Susquehanna—both for-profit and nonprofit ones—are sprouting up all over the country now. Coworking manufacturing space, commercial shared kitchens, shared advanced manufacturing centers, and textile production space are all part of the solution to ensure that small-scale manufacturing businesses can grow and succeed. The type of space you need will be dependent on what you hear from business owners in your interviews.

Zone for It

We also need zoning and permitting that allow modern manufacturing—the small-scale manufacturing businesses that are great neighbors—into our downtowns and neighborhood main streets. As discussed previously, these businesses can fill storefronts and bring energy to vacant space. They can have the retail front and give people the experience of seeing production through a window, while also selling products online or wholesale to create a more resilient balance sheet for the business.

To make sure that small-scale producers can be on Main Street, we need to amend the zoning in many places to include artisan manufacturing as a permitted land use. Then we can work with the permitting team to ensure that staff understand how to permit that use in a property zoned for commercial, mixed use, or town center (whichever zones you add the use to). A zoning variance for a specific project is fine for a quick fix, but it is likely to be a major hurdle for a small business. The amendment is important to ensure that artisan businesses can occupy commercial space by right (that is, without asking for special permission).

A number of jurisdictions changed their zoning code to accommodate this use in more places. In 2015, Nashville, Tennessee, became one of the first jurisdictions to add artisan manufacturing as a permitted land use.[3]

The ordinance adds the use to all mixed-use zones, many commercial zones, and the downtown core zone, and it specifies such use as permitted in the industrial zones, too. In 2018, Fairfax County, Virginia, passed an amendment to allow artisan manufacturing in almost all commercial zones, including production spaces up to 10,000 square feet in some locations.[4] Each location that adds this use creates more ways for small businesses to succeed and more ways for residents to build wealth in the community and thrive.

Assist with Financing for Small-Scale Manufacturers

We need to back up local small-scale manufacturing businesses with financing. These businesses aren't the boom-and-bust unicorns of tech; rather, they are often slow-growth and family-owned local businesses (no hypergrowth and quick buyouts of the businesses). They put down roots in our communities, hire from the community, and spend in the community. Yet, their capital needs are often challenging because they have upfront costs to procure the raw supplies and tools they need to make their product. Financing for product businesses become essential for growth. It may take some time to adapt existing funding sources to the needs of this sector or create new ones.

CDFIs are great partners for this financing. In many communities, the CDFIs reach small businesses that do not qualify for bank loans and that may need smaller loans than banks usually offer. For example, the Latino Economic Development Center and Washington Area Community Investment Fund are both CDFIs based in the Washington, DC, metropolitan area. They provide loans to small businesses with direct technical assistance to the business owners to help them become more financially stable and a more successful business. These mission-driven and assistance-focused organizations ensure that more people who are underrepresented in the broader financial institution support, such as Latino and Black business owners, can access the capital to grow. Local investment to launch or grow a CDFI can be essential to this kind of access.

Authorize Essential Needs Programs

Hospitals and emergency personnel struggled to find enough personal protective equipment (PPE) throughout the COVID-19 crisis in 2020. Many small-scale manufacturers pivoted nearly overnight to fill this gap and produce millions of hospital gowns, face shields, and masks. For example, the maker, academic, and small-business community in Shreveport, Louisiana, organized immediately to produce PPE for vulnerable populations in the city and the surrounding rural areas.[5] The initiative was led by the NWLA Makerspace in partnership with the Power Coalition for Equity and Justice and the local community college, with support from the city. The partnership focused on reaching residents in low-resource communities to make sure that they had proper equipment. The team worked with city leaders to make sure that outreach about the pandemic was not just online, but also directly to the community for those with lower digital access. We need to support partnerships like this one with ongoing resources, and we need to invest in other parts of our regional supply chains that can produce essential needs like PPEs.

Individual businesses are also taking up the challenge to help people with protective equipment. Stitch & Rivet, the handbag and leather goods company from chapter 1, pivoted overnight to produce beautiful face masks, both to keep the business afloat during the complete shutdown at the start of the pandemic and to make sure that its clients had the masks they needed.

Now is the time to recognize this essential need in our communities and invest in small-scale manufacturing to create the secure supply chain. There are a number of ways to achieve this goal. For example, we can provide small-scale manufacturers with grants to preserve this kind of local production capacity; after all, we already do it in other sectors. We can invest in a marketplace for small-scale manufacturers' products to help these businesses grow in nonemergency times (a great Chicago city-wide example from the private sector is SokoniStore.com). We can connect these businesses with more local procurement (as discussed earlier in this chapter). We can build stronger distributed production models (check out Xometry.com) and help more product businesses plug into that market, and we can decide to invest in this sector and the business development support it needs to help more of these businesses succeed over the long term. Most important is that we need to pick the way that serves our community best; invests in business owners from across the racial, ethnic, and income diversity of our community; and ensures that we have this capacity for the next emergency.

Communicate, Communicate, Communicate

You can combine these big pieces with the work that needs to begin now. The short-term actions can build to the big changes. Just make sure to communicate about it along the way. Show your community what is working and be clear about what didn't work in the past. Show people what is changing along the way and what kind of difference that makes for the people in your community, for your downtown, and for people's love of that place. Find the partners who can share those stories with the diverse small-business owners and the rest of your population.

Take action and do it publicly. Does a new website make the most sense? Is there a consistent message about downtown and small-scale manufacturing that needs to be shared? Can people see and celebrate the wins? How can you use each celebration to build belief and pride in that place and in those businesses? Each step here helps us do more for more people in our community and create places that people are proud of and that can thrive.

Make sure to understand where your target community spends time online. The Latino, Black, or other business owners of color may not congregate online in the same place or in the same place as White business owners. Identify these differences and work with partner organizations on the outreach. Work with civic, faith, and other neighborhood organizations to promote the information at events, on announcement boards, and through direct business owner outreach. Knoxville, Columbia, and Baltimore all have websites that feature a diversity of businesses and business owners, but they also work with partner organizations to make sure that information—both new opportunities and successes—is shared widely in the community.

Will you take on all these big ideas? The answer is no. First you need to see what the greatest needs are for small-scale manufacturers in your community. Affordable space, funding, business development support, marketing, and new relationships are all part of the equation for success, but the priorities need to be set based on what you heard from community members.

There are examples of these kinds of successes all over the country. What will you add?

Get Started Today

Some of the steps in this book might be very familiar, and some might be completely new. The personal user research interview method might make you uncomfortable. Taking a step back and looking critically at the gaps on your community—both those said clearly by those interviewed and the unspoken issues—might be hard to confront. Be uncomfortable. That's how we learn.

Be a leader. We all need your leadership, your willingness to learn, and your confidence to do something different.

Most people are not even aware of the challenges you will learn about from these conversations. Most people have no idea how to find the assets already in a community to make a big difference now. Most people do not have the tools to start closing the wealth gap or the income inequality that is our economy. But you have the ability to make the changes.

Most of all, you're not doing this alone. Communities across the United States are deciding to save their neighborhood Main Street or downtown by bringing small-scale manufacturing into the work and by changing who and how they engage people to make change happen now.

Remember that if you need help to think through the actions, Recast City is always here as a resource. Make sure to download the worksheets at www.RecastYourCity.com and answer every question or find me on LinkedIn and let me know that you read this book and have a question. And when you have successes to celebrate, I am here to celebrate with you. I can't wait to see what you make happen.

Acknowledgments

First, I want to thank you, readers, for believing in your community enough to see how you can recast your city. Thank you for believing that there can be more opportunity for your people and your downtowns, your main streets, and your neighborhood centers. Thank you for taking this on, putting in the time, and making real change happen in your community. We need more leaders like you.

Second, many, many people shared their time and energy with me to help me with this book, my business, and my career. My first thank-you has to go to the folks at the USEPA Smart Growth program and at Smart Growth America and all the staff alumni. Thank you for being such amazing people and for working with me to understand how inclusive economic development sits squarely in the center of smart growth. Thank you to Geoff Anderson, who always gave me the opportunity to figure out a new problem and invent a new solution. Thank you to Calvin Gladney, Chris Zimmerman, and the US Economic Development Administration for funding work with some of these communities and believing in it.

I also need to recognize every community that let me help. From policy changes to reinvesting in downtowns to housing and transportation options and the politics of decision-making, every place I worked over the years helped me learn more. A special thank-you goes to my clients, including Matt Anthony, Eric Avner, Bryan Berry, Jim Biggs,

Amy Bonitz, Brandy Forbes, Dawn Michelle Foster, Carrie Gartner, Evan Goldman, Liz Hagg, Susan Hart, Kelly Kline, Doug Loescher, Jair Lynch, Sarah Miller, Harrison Rue, Sue Schwartz, Tina Bingham, Adam Thies, and Mayor Dawn Zimmer, as well as the hundreds of small-scale manufacturing business owners who gave their time for an interview to make their community stronger.

Thank you to the organizations that gave me the opportunity to talk with your audiences. You gave me the space to work through many of these ideas and make the case stronger. The Smart Growth Network, National League of Cities, International Downtown Association, state main street programs, municipal leagues, state economic development associations, and all the other conference, webinar, and Facebook live event organizers helped me share how small-scale manufacturing can make a difference.

Thank you to the crew of people who cheered me on in my business and helped me through this writing project: Meredith Eaton and Katie Riess, who got me started on the book, Dena Belzer, Christopher Coes, Julia Pimsleur, Jess Randolph, Lynn Ross, Pia Silva, Jennifer Vey, Jess Zimbabwe, and so many others who shared ideas, gave me comments on chapters, and let me think out loud about it all.

Special thank-yous go to Island Press and to Heather Boyer for being a fantastic editor, encourager, and partner in bringing this passion to life; to Mike Crow at Crow Insight for suggesting illustrations for the business types and to Mary Koger for creating such amazing illustrations that I just needed to use them to open every chapter; to Stephanie Stapleton for being a great graphic designer and creating the icons for the eight elements; and to Anna Brinley for her great research and citations to help me flesh out the details.

And the biggest thank-you goes to my family for believing in me, being the most amazing cheering squad, and giving me all the support I could ever imagine to make this book a reality. Hadar, I could not have imagined a better life partner and ally. Your never-ending support and belief in me makes this all the more possible. Ana and Yoav, I thank you for being the most awesome kids, understanding that writing comes before breakfast, and inspiring me with your own tenacity. Gil and Don, I thank you for being the best brothers and cheering squad a sister could ask for. I will forever be grateful for the time that 2020 gave us to be together while I wrote this book. Papa, I thank you for everything, from believing in me always to always asking about the other 4 percent on my math test. You inspired me to reach it. And to my mother, Ruth, whom I miss every day, I thank you for being the wonderful role model, compassionate leader, and maker extraordinaire that you were.

Notes

Chapter 1　What It Means to Recast Your City

1. Specialty Food Association, "Specialty Food Sales Near $150 Billion: 2019 State of the Specialty Food Industry Report Released," Cision PR Newswire, June 4, 2019.

2. Recast City research based on sixty North American Industry Classification System codes qualifying as small-scale manufacturing jobs using national data in 2016.

3. Erika Poethig et al., "Measuring Inclusion in America's Cities," Urban Institute, April 2018.

4. Patricia Cohen, "'Still Catching Up': Jobless Numbers May Not Tell Full Story," *New York Times*, May 28, 2020.

5. Rachel Siegel and Andrew Van Dam, "U.S. Economy Contracted at Fastest Quarterly Rate on Record from April to June as Coronavirus Walloped Workers, Businesses," *Washington Post*, July 30, 2020, Economy.

6. Centers for Disease Control and Prevention, COVID-19 Hospitalization and Death by Race/Ethnicity, November 30, 2020, https://www.cdc.gov/coronavirus/2019-ncov/covid-data/investigations-discovery/hospitalization-death-by-race-ethnicity.html; Michael Sasso, "Black Business Owners' Ranks Collapse by 41% in U.S. Lockdowns," Bloomberg, June 8, 2020.

7. Neil Irwin, "America's Biggest Economic Challenge May Be Demographic Decline," *New York Times*, April 3, 2019, The Upshot.

8. Taylor Telford, "Income Inequality in America Is the Highest It's Been since Census Bureau Started Tracking It, Data Shows," *Washington Post*, September 26, 2019.

9. Jessica Semega et al., "Income and Poverty in the United States: 2018," Current Population Reports, US Census Bureau, revised June 2020, table A-4,

https://www.census.gov/content/dam/Census/library/publications/2019/demo/p60-266.pdf.

10. Patrick Sisson, "The High Cost of Abandoned Property, and How Cities Can Push Back," *Curbed*, June 1, 2018.

11. Stacy Mitchell, "Monopoly Power and the Decline of Small Business," Report on Antitrust and Entrepreneurship, American Antitrust Institute.

Chapter 2   Why We Need a New Economic Development Model

1. Mike Richard, "The Gardner Scene: It's Been 50 Years since 1970!," *Gardner News*, January 4, 2020.

2. Fortune 500, "A Database of 50 Years of FORTUNE's List of America's Largest Corporations, 1970 Full List, 1–100," accessed November 28, 2020, https://archive.fortune.com/magazines/fortune/fortune500_archive/full/1970/.

3. Carol Boyd Leon, "Occupational Winners and Losers: Who They Were during 1972–80," *Monthly Labor Review*, June 1982.

4. US Census Bureau, "1970 Census—Population, Advance Report: Final Population Counts," January 1971, revised March 23, 2016, https://www.census.gov/library/publications/1971/dec/pc-v1.

5. US Census Bureau, "Statistical Abstract of the United States: 1976," July 1976, revised July l28, 2015, https://www.census.gov/library/publications/1976/compendia/statab/97ed.html.

6. Statista Research Department, "Number of Black Owned Businesses U.S. 1972–2012," Statista, December 2015.

7. US Census Bureau, "Table 20. Population of the 100 Largest Urban Places: 1970," June 15, 1998, https://www2.census.gov/library/working-papers/1998/demo/pop-twps0027/tab20.txt.

8. Cynthia Cooper, "1970s Laws Are Today's Ammo for Women's Rights," Women's ENews, March 15, 2012.

9. Derick Moore, "U.S. Population Clock Hit 330 Million at 8:02 a.m. EDT Today Based on Population Components Measured Since 2010 Census," US Census Bureau, July 23, 2020, https://www.census.gov/library/stories/2020/07/census-bureau-estimates-united-states-population-reached-330-million-today.html#:~:text=Census%20Bureau%20Estimates%20U.S.%20Population%20Reached%20330%20Million%20Today.

10. BLS Reports, "Women in the Labor Force: A Databook, Table 2," US Bureau of Labor Statistics, December 2018, https://www.bls.gov/opub/reports/womens-databook/2018/home.htm.

11. Jens Krogstad, "Reflecting a Demographic Shift, 109 U.S. Counties Have Become Majority Nonwhite since 2000," *Pew Research Center: Fact Tank* (blog), August 21, 2019.

12. Minority Business Development Agency. "Hispanic-Owned Businesses on the Upswing." Minority Business Development Agency, December 7, 2016.

13. "Woman-Owned Businesses Are Growing 2X Faster on Average Than All Businesses Nationwide," *Business Wire*, September 23, 2019.

14. "United States Home Prices & Home Values," Zillow, 2020.

15. Gloria Guzman, "Household Income: 2018," American Community Survey Briefs, US Census Bureau, September 2019.

16. US Energy and Information Administration, "Weekly Retail Gasoline and Diesel Prices, November 2020," December 7, 2020, https://www.eia.gov/dnav/pet/pet_pri_gnd_dcus_nus_m.htm.

17. US Bureau of Labor Statistics, "Employment by Major Industry Sector," September 1, 2020.

18. Larry Buchanan, Quoctrung Bui, and Jugal K. Patel, "Black Lives Matter May Be the Largest Movement in U.S. History," *New York Times*, July 3, 2020.

19. Maria Godoy and Daniel Wood, "What Do Coronavirus Racial Disparities Look Like State by State?," NPR, May 30, 2020, https://www.npr.org/sections/health-shots/2020/05/30/865413079/what-do-coronavirus-racial-disparities-look-like-state-by-state.

20. "Inequality Books," Goodreads, 2020, https://www.goodreads.com/shelf/show/inequality.

21. Sam Raskin, "Amazon's HQ2 Deal with New York, Explained," *Curbed NY*, February 14, 2019. With specific details: $897 million from the city's Relocation and Employment Assistance Program, $386 million from the Industrial and Commercial Abatement Program, an additional $505 million in a capital grant, and $1.2 billion in "Excelsior" credits if its job creation goals are met.

22. Carl Davis, "Tax Incentives: Costly for States, Drag on the Nation," Institute on Taxation and Economic Policy, August 14, 2013.

23. Philip Mattera, Kasia Tarczynska, and Greg LeRoy, "Megadeals: The Largest Economic Development Subsidy Packages Ever Awarded by State and Local Governments in the United States," *Good Jobs First*, June 2013.

24. Margaret J. Krauss, "Snagging Amazon HQ2: Who Wins When Tax Subsidies Lure Big Business To PA?," WESA, October 19, 2017.

25. Ally Schweitzer, "D.C. Gives Tech Companies Millions of Dollars in Tax Breaks. Are They Worth It?," *WAMU* (blog), December 3, 2018.

26. Craig Howard and Natalia Carrizosa, "Review of Montgomery County's Economic Development Incentive Program," Office of Legislative Oversight, Report No. 2013-2, 2013.

27. Montgomery Planning, "Montgomery County Trends: A Look at People, Housing, and Jobs," 2019.

28. David Dayen, "Amazon Is Thriving Thanks to Taxpayer Dollars," Good Jobs First, January 9, 2018.

29. Timothy J. Bartik and John C. Austin, "Most Business Incentives Don't Work. Here's How to Fix Them," *Brookings* (blog), November 1, 2019.

30. Richard Florida, "High-Tech Startups Are Still Concentrated in Just a Few Cities," *CityLab*, October 13, 2017.

31. Sophie Quinton,. "Black Businesses Largely Miss Out on Opportunity Zone Money," Pewtrusts.org, June 24, 2020.

32. Brett Theodos et al., "An Early Assessment of Opportunity Zones for Equitable Development Projects," Urban Institute, 2020.

33. Taylor Telford "Income Inequality in America Is the Highest It's Been since Census Bureau Started Tracking It, Data Shows," *Washington Post*, September 26, 2019.

34. Dionissi Aliprantis and Daniel R. Carroll, "What Is Behind the Persistence of the Racial Wealth Gap?," Federal Reserve Bank of Cleveland, February 28, 2019, https://www.clevelandfed.org/newsroom-and-events/publications/economic-commentary/2019-economic-commentaries/ec-201903-what-is-behind-the-persistence-of-the-racial-wealth-gap.aspx.

35. Aliprantis and Carroll, "What Is Behind the Persistence."

36. Elise Gould and Valerie Wilson, "Black Workers Face Two of the Most Lethal Preexisting Conditions for Coronavirus—Racism and Economic Inequality," *Economic Policy Institute* (blog), June 1, 2020.

37. Pew Research Center, "Demographic and Economic Data, by Race," chap. 3 of *King's Dream Remains an Elusive Goal; Many Americans See Racial*

Disparities, Pew Research Center Social and Demographic Trends Project (blog), August 22, 2013.

38. Rakesh Kochhar and Anthony Cilluffo, "Racial and Ethnic Income Inequality in America: 5 Key Findings," *Pew Research Center* (blog), July 12, 2018.

39. Gould and Wilson, "Black Workers Face Two of the Most Lethal Preexisting Conditions."

40. Gould and Wilson, "Black Workers Face Two of the Most Lethal Preexisting Conditions."

41. Hannah Knowles, "Number of Working Black Business Owners Falls 40%, Far More than Other Groups amid Coronavirus," *Seattle Times*, May 25, 2020.

42. Alana Semuels, "When Wall Street Is Your Landlord," *The Atlantic*, February 13, 2019.

43. Building the Field of Community Engagement partners and Tracy Babler, "Distinguish Your Work: Outreach or Community Engagement? An Assessment Tool," 2014.

44. Knowledge Leader Editor, "The Changing Face of America's Malls," *Colliers Commercial Real Estate* (blog), December 18, 2018.

45. Urban Institute and Brookings Institution, "The State of State (and Local) Tax Policy Briefing Book," 2020, https://www.taxpolicycenter.org/briefing-book/how-do-state-and-local-sales-taxes-work.

46. Lauren Thomas, "Gap, Tesla and Victoria's Secret Are among the Nearly 5,000 Store Closings Already in 2019," CNBC, March 9, 2019.

47. Kris Hudson and Ann Zimmerman, "Mall Glut to Clog Market for Years," *Wall Street Journal*, September 10, 2008, Real Estate.

48. Paul Mackun and Steven Wilson, "Population Distribution and Change: 2000 to 2010," US Census Bureau, C2010BR-01, 2011.

49. Kevin Cody, Alexander Levy, and Robin Trantham, "CoStar Market Analysis: Three Trends Driving the Retail Market Today," CoStar Insights, November 12, 2019.

50. Steve McLinden, "Retail Is the Vital Hub for Successful Mixed-Use Development, Experts Say," International Council of Shopping Centers, May 30, 2018.

51. Paula Munger, "Barriers to Apartment Construction Index," National Apartment Association, April 23, 2019.

Chapter 3   A Stronger Economic Development Model with Small-Scale Manufacturing

1. Thrillist Travel, "America's Best Small Cities to Move to Before They Get Too Popular," Thrillist, September 28, 2018.

2. National Complete Streets Coalition, "Complete Streets Stimulate the Local Economy," 2020.

3. Ian Duncan, "Study Finds Deep Racial Disparities in Way Baltimore Allocates Public Construction Dollars," *Baltimore Sun*, December 12, 2017, https://www.baltimoresun.com/maryland/baltimore-city/bs-md-ci-capital -budget-race-inequality-20171211-story.html.

4. Grist Creative, "Fighting for the Soul of Little Haiti in Miami," Marguerite Casey Foundation, March 10, 2020.

5. Jodi Mailander Farrell, "Now's the Time to Visit Little Haiti, on the Brink of Change," Visit Florida, https://www.visitflorida.com/en-us/cities/miami/ visit-little-haiti-in-miami.html, accessed November 24, 2020.

6. Ariana P. Torres, Maria I. Marshall, and Sandra Sydnor, "Does Social Capital Pay Off? The Case of Small Business Resilience after Hurricane Katrina," Journal of Contingencies and Crisis Management 27(2): 168–81.

7. Ariana P. Torres, Maria I. Marshall, and Sandra Sydnor, "Does Social Capital Pay Off? The Case of Small Business Resilience after Hurricane Katrina," *Journal of Contingencies and Crisis Management* 27(2): 168–81.

8. Endeavor Insight, "The Power of Entrepreneur Networks," Partnership for New York City, 2014, http://www.nyctechmap.com/nycTechReport.pdf.

9. Knight Foundation, "Soul of the Community 2010: Overall Findings," 2010.

10. Knight Foundation, "Soul of the Community."

11. National Association of Realtors, "National Smart Growth Frequencies: 2017 Topline Results," American Strategies, 2017.

12. M. Leanne Lachman and Deborah L. Brett, *Gen Y and Housing: What They Want and Where They Want It* (Washington, DC: Urban Land Institute, 2015).

13. Stacy Mitchell, "The Economic Impact of Locally Owned Businesses vs. Chains: A Case Study in Midcoast Maine," Institute for Local Self-Reliance, September 1, 2003.

14. BBB, "10 Ways Small Businesses Benefit Their Local Communities," Medium, April 23, 2019, https://medium.com/@BBBNWP/10-ways-small-businesses -benefit-their-local-communities-7273380c90a9.

15. Andersonville Chamber of Commerce, "Retail Attraction and Market Research," 2012, http://www.andersonville.org/business-resources/retail-attraction-market-research/.

16. N. Cambria et al., *Segregation in St. Louis: Dismantling the Divide* (St. Louis, MO: Washington University, 2018).

17. Emily Badger, "More Segregated Cities Spend Less on Parks, Roads and Sewers," *Washington Post*, October 28, 2015.

18. Andre M. Perry and David Harshberger, "America's Formerly Redlined Neighborhoods Have Changed, and so Must Solutions to Rectify Them." *Brookings Institution* (blog), October 14, 2019.

19. Anna Brinley and Ann Hilbig, "How a Houston, Texas Neighborhood Center Is Using Diversity to Strengthen a Neighborhood," *Brookings Institution* (blog), October 4, 2019.

20. Here We Grow NC, "Marion Initiative Revives Downtown Business," April 2019, https://herewegrownc.org/local-stories-list/marion-initiative-revives-downtown-business/.

21. John Kotter, "Tailored Leadership Development." Kotterinc.com, 2020, https://www.kotterinc.com/strategies-we-help-accelerate/tailored-leadership-development/.

Chapter 4   Five Steps to Recast Your City

1. US Census Bureau, Quick Facts, Columbia City, Missouri, Population Estimates, July 1, 2019, https://www.census.gov/quickfacts/columbiacity missouri.

Chapter 5   Step 1: Light the Spark

1. Johan E. Korteling, Anne-Marie Brouwer, and Alexander Toet, "A Neural Network Framework for Cognitive Bias," *Frontiers in Psychology* 9 (September 2018).

Chapter 7   Step 3: Start the Conversation and Get Great Information from Your Interviews

1. Mona Yang, "The Essential Guide to User Research," Medium, September 1, 2020.

2. Susan Farrell, "UX Research Cheat Sheet," Nielsen Norman Group, February 12, 2017.

3. Ben Ralph, "Intro to UX Research," Medium, February 13, 2017.

Chapter 8   Step 4: Analyze the Input and Understand What It All Means

1. Cre[8], "Things Are Made Here," accessed November 24, 2020, http://www.comomakes.com/.
2. The Loop, accessed November 24, 2020, https://theloopcomo.com/.
3. See, for example, Brad Feld's *Startup Communities: Building an Entrepreneurial Ecosystem in Your City*, 2nd ed. (New York: Wiley, 2020), for a great resource on building a business community.

Chapter 9   Step 5: Be Impatient and Act Now

1. Jill Rosen and Katie Pearce, "Johns Hopkins Makes Diversity a Cornerstone of New HopkinsLocal Goals," The Hub, Johns Hopkins University, January 29, 2020.
2. John Joyce, "Calling All Entrepreneurs: This 'Reverse Pitch' Is for You," *Triad Business Journal*, November 5, 2019.
3. Metropolitan Government of Nashville, "Ordinance No. BL2015-1121," last modified July 22, 2015, https://www.nashville.gov/mc/ordinances/term_2011_2015/bl2015_1121.htm.
4. Tony Castrilli, "New Zoning Rules Open Shop Doors for Craft Manufacturing in Fairfax County," Public Affairs, Fairfax County, Virginia, December 5, 2018.
5. Jennifer Blakeslee, "Plan C Live: Community Impact of Covid-19 in Northwest Louisiana," Make: Community, August 18, 2020, https://www.youtube.com/watch?v=1jtZuiFltUE&feature=emb_logo.

About the Author

Ilana Preuss is the founder and chief executive officer of Recast City. She is the coauthor of *Discovering Your City's Maker Economy* and *Made in Place: Small-Scale Manufacturing and Neighborhood Revitalization*, as well as a chapter author for *Creative Placemaking* and *Sustainable Nation*. She is a TEDx speaker on "The Economic Power of Great Places" and a featured keynote speaker.

Preuss's passion for great places grew out of her experience working with big and small cities all over the United States

Aimee Custis Photography

when she led the technical assistance program at the US Environmental Protection Agency's Smart Growth Program and as the vice president and chief of staff at Smart Growth America. She holds a bachelor of arts degree in urban and regional studies from Cornell University and a master of city planning degree from the University of Maryland.

When Preuss is not working with a city or coaching a community leader, she can be found cooking up a storm with her two amazing teenagers. She lives in Maryland, always hunts down the local chocolate production business when onsite for a project, and still sings along to eighties music with her husband and kids.